TEN STEPS
to
PUBLISHING CHILDREN'S BOOKS

How to Develop, Revise, & Sell All Kinds of Books for Children

by Berthe Amoss and Eric Suben

WRITER'S DIGEST BOOKS
Cincinnati, Ohio

Ten Steps to Publishing Children's Books — How to Develop, Revise, & Sell All Kinds of Books for Children
© 1997 by Berthe Amoss and Eric Suben
Printed in Hong Kong by More Than A Card, Inc.
Published by Writer's Digest Books, an imprint of F&W Publications, Inc., 1507 Dana Avenue, Cincinnati, Ohio, 45207.
1-800-289-0963
First Edition

Library of Congress Catalog-in-Publication Data

Amoss, Berthe.
    Ten steps to publishing children's books : how to develop, revise & sell all kinds of books for children / by Berthe Amoss and Eric Suben. -- 1st ed.
        p.   cm.
    Includes index.
    ISBN 0-89879-805-1 (alk. paper)
    1. Children's literature--Authorship. 2. Children's literature--Marketing.
I. Suben, Eric. II. Title
PN147.5.A47   1997
808.06'8--dc21

This hardcover edition of *Ten Steps to Writing and Illustrating Children's Books* features a "self jacket" that eliminates the need for a separate dust jacket. It provides sturdy protection for your book while it saves paper, trees and energy.

The authors and publisher have made every effort to trace the ownership of all copyrighted material reproduced in this book. They now acknowledge and thank the following individuals and entities for permission to use such materials:
        Harry N. Abrams, Inc.
        Aladdin Books
        Elizabeth Robeau Amoss
        Mike Artell
        Bantam Doubleday Dell Publishing Group, Inc.
        Bullfinch Press
        Coward-McCann, Inc.
        Richard Egielski
        Farrar, Straus and Giroux
        G.P. Putnam's Sons
        Chuck Galey
        Joan Elizabeth Goodman
        Harcourt Brace & Company
        HarperCollins Publishers
        Barbara Shook Hazen
        Hyperion Books for Children
        Katie Lee
        Lerner Publications Company
        Little Simon
        Emily Arnold McCully
        The New Yorker Magazine
        Joan Lowery Nixon
        Oxford University Press
        Pantheon Books
        Penguin Books USA
        Richard Peck
        Amye Rosenberg
        Whitney Stewart
        Trudy Corporation
        Western Publishing Company, Inc.
        William Morrow
        Beth Woods
        Writer's Digest Books

Edited by Jack Heffron
Written by Berthe Amoss and Eric Suben
Interior design by Rebecca Blake
Cover design and collage by Rebecca Blake
Cover illustrations by Berthe Amoss

Table of Contents

Introduction

There is an old canard that goes: You can't teach writing because writers are born and not made. The truth is that nature plays a lesser role than nurture, and that if you're reading this book, chances are great you already have the talent, otherwise known as a yearning, to create a book for children.

In *Ten Steps to Publishing Children's Books*, we want to present what very definitely can be taught: the essential knowledge and skills you need to get your book published.

We start with you, helping you to assess your ability, interests, and experience in terms of where you are now and what your goals are. Then we explore the many categories of children's books to help you find your niche. We bring the marketplace to you, describing the opportunities in the teeming children's book field, and finally, we show you how to get and hold a place in the market by putting yourself in a position to meet other writers, agents and editors.

Our experience, as our editor once put it, comes from both sides of the desk: the author/illustrator's and the publisher/editor's. Although we share a love of children's books and a long association with them, our diverse experience gives us "Two Perspectives," the name we've given to our workshops and the subtitle of our books. We believe our different viewpoints will enrich your perspective and increase your options along the road to success.

Another strong, shared belief of ours is that you will learn most by studying case histories, the stories of how well-known writers and illustrators were successful in meeting challenges and getting published. We have used case histories throughout our book, but the icing on the cake is Step 10 in which successful, well-known writers and illustrators have contributed essays telling you in their own words how they first came to be published.

Beyond grammar and style, there are very few rules in writing, but we will give you guidelines and advice and ideas.

You may have thought: Someday I'm going to write that story I tell the kids and try to get it pub-

lished. But you never seem to find the time – besides you don't know how to go about getting it published. Or, maybe you have written your story; in fact, you have been writing stories for some time and have enough rejection slips to paper a wall. You're wondering what in the world those publishers want.

Have faith! Most people have no idea what goes on behind the scenes in publishing – you are in the majority. Of all the writers we know, few have succeeded on the first try. The exception is Beverly Cleary, who submitted *Ramona* to an editor who only had to "move a few commas around" before publishing it. Most are like Madeleine L'Engle, who submitted *A Wrinkle in Time* twenty-one times before it was accepted.

This book is meant to give you an understanding of the complete process of creating a book for children so you can bring yours all the way to acceptance. Here's our step-by-step, easy-to-follow approach: Step 1 is to analyze your own strengths and skills in terms of where you are now and what your goals are. Step 2 is to explore the many categories of children's books in order to see where you fit in. Step 3 is to target your audience. Steps 4 and 5 are to approach the entire book as an art form, or to put it commercially, as an irresistible product. In Steps 6 and 7, you study the real world of the marketplace to see what's available and how you can take advantage of opportunities. In Step 8 we'll show you how to rethink your story in case you're stalemated and turn it into the one an editor wants to publish. In Step 9, we'll tell you all about agents, editors, publishers, what they're looking for, and how to give it to them. In Step 10, well-known authors and illustrators tell you the steps they took to reach success.

Each step along the road to publishing is peppered with reading suggestions, advice, case histories, checklists and exercises identified by logos for easy reference. You will be learning and writing a publishable manuscript as you go, avoiding the common pitfalls, most of which we, your authors, fell into when we started out!

You can make the publishing process work for you and find your niche by exploring the many minimarkets and categories. The place for you may be nonfiction, periodicals, poetry, drama, illustration only, paper engineering, the young adult novel, picture books, etc. We'll describe the opportunities to cultivate assignment writing, writing for licensed characters, writing for the enormous educational market with all of its special categories. And, perhaps most important of all, we'll show you how you can be creative and proactive in pioneering markets for the book you want to write. We provide a guide to writers' conferences, etiquette with editors, and stories

of how membership in groups and participation in activities worked for many real-life authors.

In our first book, *Writing and Illustrating Children's Books for Publication*, we spent a great deal of time on the actual mechanics of writing and illustrating. Review some of this material if, after you analyze your strengths and weaknesses, you discover you need more information about the craft of writing. However, this book is intended to guide you through the potholes of publication by an in-depth, unique approach to you as craftsman and the marketplace as your field of opportunity.

We offer you thirty years of our combined experience: Berthe's dozen picture books, four young adult novels, twelve years of teaching children's literature and writing a newspaper column on children's books plus Eric's nine years of editing in a major publishing house and writing more than thirty picture books. In addition, we have worked six years together conducting writing workshops and teaching.

There's a well-known story about Ursula Nordstrom, the legendary editor of Harper & Row in the sixties, who discovered Margaret Wise Brown (*Goodnight Moon*), Maurice Sendak (*Where the Wild Things Are*) and other great authors and illustrators. Ursula Nordstrom was asked, "How is it that you, without a college education, feel qualified to decide which children's books should be published?" The famous editor answered, "I am a former child."

All of us are too, and if we could just look at the world as we once did, armed with the knowledge and skills offered here, we'd succeed in giving children the best of books, the kind that help them develop and find meaning in life.

And so, we invite you to follow these ten steps all the way to acceptance.

Who Are You?

T he first step toward getting published is knowing who you are. Of course you know your name and background. But we mean knowing what makes you specially qualified to write books for children, what kinds of children's books you are qualified to write, and what kind of special ability, skill or quality you can offer to turn on publishers. Analyze yourself in terms of your interests, education and special training.

As you get started, take a good look at your background, training and experience. When you do, you may be concerned your credentials do not equip you to write for children. If so, think about some of the famous children's authors and illustrators and their careers before children's books. Some started out as well-known people; some led more everyday lives.

- Kay Thompson (*Eloise*) was a Hollywood performer, Judy Garland's vocal coach and Liza Minnelli's godmother;

EXERCISE

Write down the answers to these questions:

- *What skills do you have in general?*
- *What did you study in school?*
- *What do you do for a living?*
- *What are your hobbies/interests?*
- *What can you offer children as an author?*
- *What can you offer a publisher?*
- *What writing and/or illustration skills do you have?*
- *What sales and/or marketing skills do you have?*

You need to think about and answer all these questions to confront and conquer the challenge of writing for children and getting published.

CASE HISTORY (ERIC)

People enter the field of children's books from many different starting points. When I was a young man, I was looking for a job – any job – in publishing. I got one at Golden Books. I was hooked the day I walked into the archives and happened across a copy of The Lion's Paw, *illustrated by Gustaf Tenggren, a Little Golden Book I had loved as a small child and forgotten completely until that truly Proustian moment. I found many such opportunities to revisit and understand my own childhood. They so moved me that I have remained connected with children's publishing for many years.*

- Peggy Parish (*Amelia Bedelia*) was a teacher at the Dalton School in New York City;
- Beverly Cleary (*Ramona the Pest, Henry Huggins*) was a librarian;
- Beni Montresor (*May I Bring a Friend?*) is a set and costume designer for the operatic stage;
- Kenneth Grahame (*The Wind in the Willows*) was a bank clerk.

The point is, your credentials need not be specifically related to children or children's books. But you do need a lively interest in the world around you and a willingness to follow up any opportunity that comes your way.

In our classes and workshops, we have had people from many walks of life who wanted to, and were equipped to, create books for children – lawyers, professors, teachers, professional storytellers, performance artists, screenwriters, homemakers, journalists, retirees, librarians, doctors. Often, aspiring children's-book writers are professionals who work with children as educators, counselors or parents. Just as often, they are people whose work involves significant amounts of writing and language – for instance, lawyers or librarians. What makes people want to write for children may differ in each case. Many people start because they are parents and grandparents used to telling stories to the children in their families. A father may make up a story, and his young ones may love it, and he may want to spread it around to others. A.A. Milne (*Winnie-the-Pooh*) was one such, and Edward Ardizzone not only wrote but illustrated the wonderful Lucy and Tim books for his own children.

CASE HISTORY (ERIC)

When I was just beginning to edit my own list of books and develop relationships with authors, I had dinner with a writer whose work I greatly admired and wanted to publish. Dinner was exhausting! The author told endless stories and anecdotes, one more improbable than the next. Stories about meeting and traveling with royalty and movie stars, stories about faraway places and being sought after by film buffs and world-renowned figures. From my own experiences, I know that people lead improbable lives. But I had another insight as I digested this dinner – this gifted writer was a storyteller. Story was his passion and his art and what he did for a living. No surprise, then, that dinner with him was what the author Christina Stead called "an ocean of story."

9

CASE HISTORY (ERIC)

The importance of the child within may be shown by the things you treasure. One boss of mine kept a tiny sneaker, just big enough for a two-year-old, on the bookshelf in her office. In my office, I always had my original copy of Harold and the Purple Crayon, *bought with allowance money at a Scholastic Book Fair when I was in the early primary grades. The book held up to multiple readings at all stages of my life. When I came to study the works of Pirandello at UCLA, I thought, "Aha, Harold!" The book shows how we create our own reality – one of the great themes of modernist literature- – and that idea has perhaps never been as cogently expressed as it is in Crockett Johnson's magical little book.*

Many children's-book authors and illustrators are overgrown children; many are compulsive storytellers. It is not one reason or quality that makes a person a children's-book author; but there are some common denominators: love of language; sensitivity to art and illustration; an ability to connect with the child in oneself; a desire to communicate something, to tell a story, to make young eyes sparkle with wonder.

One important quality is the ability to be in touch with your "child within." You do not need contact with and access to lots of actual children to have the right point of view for children's writing. You need access to yourself as a child, the things you thought, did and wondered, the words you knew, the books you loved. When you have developed that point of view and begun to translate it into writing, you will see that writing for children seems a natural expression of yourself, though you are an adult.

We expect that you come to this book as someone who struggles with the challenge of writing. Writing for children admittedly poses some challenges not faced by writers for an adult audience: conveying complex thoughts in simple language and sentences; choosing appropriate subject matter; considering the myriad format choices and production possibilities available in children's books. We address these aspects in later steps in this book, starting with Step 2 on formats. But right now you can prepare to meet these challenges by reading and absorbing as much as possible from published books for children. First, be aware of the something special you want to communicate. Then work on clothing the something special in language that will help it reach the right audience.

If you're serious about being published,

EXERCISE

Write down why you want to write for children, and be as honest as you can. Here are some thoughts:
- *I love children*
- *I love to write*
- *I want to make more money*
- *I see a gap in the children's-book marketplace*
- *There are no books out there on my subject matter*

Write down at least five reasons. Then rank them in order. Keep them posted near your workplace, to remind yourself when you become discouraged.

think about what brings you to the world of children's writing. Understanding your motivation will suggest what next steps you need to take in order to succeed. If you have a very specific goal, like the author of the story about her son's disability (see page 12), recognize there may be a restricted market for your work and focus your selling efforts appropriately (see Step 7).

If you have been telling stories to your own children and grandchildren and think the stories could succeed beyond the family circle, recognize the stories may need to be made more universal and polished quite a bit before they will be suitable for the competitive publishing marketplace (see Step 8). If you illustrate, you must analyze the relative strengths of your prose and your pictures and take appropriate steps to strengthen the weaker skill.

You can start to know what and how you should write by looking at what you read. What do you like most about what you read? Think about the books you like best. What is it that you like about them? If it's a strong narrative voice, think about writing in first person. If it's elegant descriptions, maybe you should be writing longer fiction for young readers where you can really expand.

Understanding what you like will help you play to your strengths because you will write best what you like best. Think about *Jane Eyre*. The story is told in the first person, and the reader is pulled in by Jane's narrative voice on the very first page. By page 10, the reader is completely under the spell of this extraordinary character, and of the author who captures her voice so perfectly. Now think about a writer like Margaret Wise Brown (*Goodnight Moon*, *The Runaway Bunny*), who can write on a level of pure abstraction and create a story through her magical use of language and free-associative writing. One would almost need to be a poet to do what she did so

CASE HISTORY (ERIC)

Don't be ashamed if one primary motivation is pecuniary.(However, you should recognize that money in children's books is slow to come and slow to build into anything significant.) I was once negotiating for the juvenile publishing rights to the wonderful PBS series Wild America. *Marty Stouffer, the naturalist, wildlife photographer and creator and host of the show, is a devoted father and was genuinely delighted with the idea of generating children's books. But he also said wryly, "And I wouldn't mind if I make five dollars out of it, either." If you've done your work carefully and well, you should be paid for it!*

CASE HISTORY (ERIC)

I once wrote a book because of something omitted from a book I had read. In a children's book about a mommy returning to work, the little girl said, "But when will we be together?" Mommy replied that the family would spend time together on Saturday. But the story ended on Friday, and Saturday never came. I was dying of curiosity about what the family did on Saturday, so my next book became The Busy Saturday Word Book, *where a different family did all kinds of neat things on a Saturday. My motivation was finding out the answer to the question left unanswered by the first author!*

CASE HISTORY

An attorney and law professor attending one of our classes was moved to write for children after her young son was severely injured in a backyard accident. Her son's resulting disability made tasks that were routine for some children into challenges for him. For instance, tying his shoelaces and dressing himself became very special accomplishments. What drove the author to write this story was the idea that young children could understand her son's disability through reading a story about the obstacles he faced every day. Her story also touched the universal chord of allowing children to revisit their own attempts to master tasks and come to terms with their own challenges.

well, to understand the internal workings of language and create a structure out of the sounds of words. Which kind of writing is more "you"?

Once you analyze and understand your reasons for writing for children and your strengths as a writer, you will develop confidence in your ability to write children's books for publication. Of course, this feeling of confidence comes only through hard work – working at understanding the unique demands of children's books, polishing your writing till it shines, exploring the marketplace and selling your "product." If you've done the work and feel the confidence, you will be able to express that good feeling in every contact you have with publishers. And your confidence in yourself will create a feeling of confidence in you and your work.

Your strength may not be the actual writing. If so, build on the qualities and expertise you do have, and let those be your source of confidence. Everyone who sets out to write for children is not a great writer. Dinah L. Moché writes prose that does not sparkle. But she is a Ph.D. in astronomy and keeps in touch with actual children by going to activities that involve them with her subject matter, like NASA space camp. Her books are outstanding sellers not because of her writing but because she combines hard knowledge with sensitivity to children's interests and concerns. Judy Blume (*Blubber, Superfudge*) is another good example of a successful writer whose writing has rough edges but whose understanding of young people's emotions and tastes is without parallel.

Like these writers, you have to find out what your strengths are. How can you determine who you are with respect to writing children's books? You may start out without having thought much about children's books –

CASE HISTORY (ERIC)

People who want to write children's books may come from the unlikeliest backgrounds. One day Shere Hite telephoned my office at Golden Books. Ms. Hite is the author of top-selling studies about adult sexuality (for instance, The Hite Report*). One reason why her books sell so well is that they are very explicit and filled with salacious detail. Of course, most editors of adult books would be tickled pink to be called up by a famous, best-selling author. Although Ms. Hite was an unknown quantity as a writer for children, I was intrigued and asked her to send her story. It was no steamy adult opus, but a rather sweet story about Ms. Hite's pet dog.*

you may be more interested in sophisticated modernist literature and your head may be far from the world of children. You may be amazed at how much mature editors seem to know about children and what interests them. But you can master this information. Few, if any, editors have degrees in child psychology. They just absorb information through long exposure to the literature. You do not need to have specialized study in the field of chil-

dren's books and literature, or even children, to succeed. But you must be willing to do the hard work it takes to understand the audience, the technical demands and the aesthetic requirements of the medium. Get to know children's books – read, read, read!

Your confidence will help you build skill in marketing your work and yourself. This means belief in your "product," persistence and following up all opportunities and contacts that come your way. You may have difficulty with this step on the road to success if you are a shy person or someone without confidence in your work. But you can – and must – overcome these obstacles to succeed. You can achieve confidence by knowing your manuscript is the best it can be, that your submission reflects thorough research and knowledge of the marketplace, and that you have the tools to tailor your work to the publisher's needs. Subsequent steps in this book will show you how to scale the heights to publication. But even after you have finished this book, research, study and careful self-editing will help you know your manuscript is presented absolute-

ly professionally, demonstrating knowledge of language, age groups and formats. You can also make sure your work constitutes a viable submission for each publisher you target by

EXERCISE

Perhaps the most systematic way to arrive at who you are with respect to writing children's books for publication is to subdivide the question and explore your qualifications from several different points of view. Make a grid that looks like this: In the upper left-hand block list your strengths as a writer. Here include your professional credentials. In the upper right-hand block, put down your marketing strengths, including personal characteristics that set you apart from others. In the lower left-hand corner, make a list of your contacts. Finally, save the lower right-hand block for areas to improve. We will explore each of these categories of information in later steps in the book, but you can start filling in your writing strengths here and now. Revise this grid as you make progress through the ten steps to acceptance. We believe you will add to the list of writing strengths as you go along!

spending time on market research. Leave nothing to chance – but when chance opens a door, be ready to step inside.

What personal skills and attributes do you bring to the challenge of presenting your work for publication? You need persistence and the ability to turn out a professional-looking product every time you send your material for consideration. If you will be meeting with editors and delivering your work in person, you must look good as well. If you get nervous in extemporaneous settings, script your presentation to publishers. You should be very familiar with your own experience and motivation and with your own credits so that these are ready on your tongue as you present yourself and your work.

Your contacts are really a type of sales and marketing strength. You may know more people than you think who are involved with the world of publishing and specifically with publishing children's books. Developing these contacts is Step 7 in this book. But for now, think of anyone you know who has ever been commercially published. Try to get the names of their contacts. Join a writer's group or get an agent – these affiliations will help you meet people. You can develop your own contacts by attending writers' conferences; but also by approaching editors in a professional and pleasant manner in your correspondence and telephone contacts. See Step 6 for more on these topics.

You probably know people with connections to writing, books, publishing and illustration. You almost certainly know people involved with children's concerns as educators, librarians, counselors or social workers. Think of

CHECKLIST

Rank the following in order of strength:
- *My education and background*
- *My writing*
- *My personality*
- *My reasons for wanting to write children's books*

The one strongest thing is what you should emphasize. You can put that aside now and start to concentrate on strengthening the other aspects of your children's book persona.

CASE HISTORY (BERTHE)

Luck plays a huge part in getting published. But luck is worth little if you don't make the most of it. After several books with Harper & Row, I received a rejection. Not knowing what to do, I went to a bank of pay phones and began to call around to publishers for an appointment. A woman at the next telephone overheard me and said, "Why not call Alvin Tresselt at Parents Magazine Press? I used to work for him, and he's very nice." I did call him, and he published six of my books. I've always thought of that woman at the next phone as my guardian angel. Do not look askance at serendipity!

anyone and everyone you know – a schoolteacher, a local newspaper reporter – who is involved with books or writing in any professional capacity. These people are the start of your publishing world. Tell them what you're doing and solicit their advice. Chances are they know people, and those people know people. Eventually, you will find yourself connected to the big world of book publishing. But you have to get the ball rolling and not let it drop.

If you have been following the exercises and stories in this chapter, you will by now have written down lists of your education, work background, writing interests and skills, and some personality traits. Analyzing these lists should help you identify and focus on the subject matter and skills that will work for you in your writing and also in marketing and selling yourself and your work to publishers. As you analyze these facets of the package that is you, you can begin to get a handle on your gimmick and work it to your advantage.

One key aspect of marketing is knowing to whom you will market your product. You can find out about publishers from directories to the publishing industry, like *Literary Market Place* and *Writer's Market* or the home page of the Children's Book Council.

An excellent source of information is your own bookstore or library. Carefully

CASE HISTORY (ERIC)

Often it is the luck of finding just the right editor that results in the acceptance of a story. When I was a young child, my father did not read to me and my brother at bedtime--he played the guitar and sang folk songs. One favorite was the song about the fox:

> The fox went out on a chilly night;
> He prayed to the moon for to give him light.
> He'd many miles to run that night,
> Before he reached the town-o, town-o, town-o…

This old song had been adapted into a famous book by Peter Spier. But when artist Nina Barbaresi presented her version with an Old American twist, I couldn't resist the chance to publish it in honor of my dad. Nina's finding an editor with a weak spot for this song was pure chance!

note the books you pick up when visiting such venues. Do you repeatedly pick up books published by particular publishers? If so, you may be recognizing a quality in their books that exists also in your work. This insight should be the beginning of your list of potential recipients of your submission. But don't stop with the publishers you like. Look at all the books and educate yourself about the children's-book market in terms of who publishes what.

Finally, remember there may be no greater quality for getting published than luck. Luck is not dumb chance. It is something you attract by being attentive to opportunities around you, by being unashamed of your objective, by wrapping yourself in a cloak of children's-book karma. The more you read, think and write children's books, the more you will talk about them. Each action and word of yours is like a pebble in a pond – there is a ripple effect you cannot calculate. After you start to make your interest known, people will start to bring you information about children's books and publishing. After you absorb that information and start to act on it, you will start to meet people connected with the publishing world or recognize that you already know such people. Do the hard work outlined in this book. But at the same time, keep your eyes and ears open – the world of publishing children's books is all around you. You have but to jump into it!

READING LIST

Each of these books tells you something about a celebrated author and the things that made him or her write books for young people:

- The Making of Goodnight Moon *by Leonard S. Marcus*
- A Circle of Quiet *by Madeleine L'Engle*
- A Girl from Mayhill *by Beverly Cleary*
- Surprised by Joy *by C.S. Lewis*
- Invincible Louisa *by Cornelia Meigs*
- The Enchanted Places *by Christopher Milne*
- A History of the Writings of Beatrix Potter *by Leslie Linder*
- Boy *by Roald Dahl*

Also look for Dreamchild, *a wonderful videotape about Lewis Carroll and the real Alice.*

Investigating the Categories

Now that you've analyzed your strengths and skills, you may find that this chapter about categories is the most important step in our book. Its goal is to help you see where you fit into the field of children's literature; if you find your niche, you're more than halfway to acceptance by a publisher.

But, have you ever noticed that the best books for children defy categories? *Charlotte's Web*, *The Adventures of Huckleberry Finn*, *A Christmas Carol*, *Robinson Crusoe*, to name a few classics, refuse to fit into neat little groupings; they spill over into different genres, age levels, and subject matter. It is annoying to those of us who are trying to understand why they work, but it is also illuminating because uniqueness is at the heart of creativity and the classics.

ROBINSON 1719

Take *Charlotte's Web* as an example. It begins with realism: Fern, a farmer's daughter wants to save a runt pig, and we see the situation from Fern's point of view. E.B. White could very well have written the whole book true to life about a sensitive young girl growing up on a farm where the animals she loves are raised for slaughter. A lesser writer might have done so, but White leaves Fern's story and takes us into the barnyard where the animals are talking! What is this book, fact or fantasy? It breaks all the rules! And who's the audience? A precocious four-year-old, a middle reader or you? Classics are for all ages!

Then there's *Robinson Crusoe*, which Daniel Defoe wrote as a political satire for adults. Children grabbed it for themselves and, thanks to their demand, it has never been out of print. Mark Twain said he wrote *Huckleberry Finn* for children, but university professors of English have borrowed it from children's literature and it is often spoken of as "the great American novel."

And so, if it is true that good books defy categories, what is the use of categories to you? The thing to be said in favor of organizing books into groups is that it brings a measure of clarity to a confusing, vast field and helps you to understand the possibilities open to

Case History (Berthe)

When I was teaching children's literature at Tulane, I hated dividing books into categories, but it was the only way I knew of making teaching order out of the marvelously diverse world of children's books. I worried the boundaries were too fuzzy in reality but too rigid in theory, and I thought they might inhibit the students' enthusiastic creativity for producing their own books as a final project. But every semester brought a fresh batch of delightful, often publishable, illustrated picture books, interactive books, chapter books and occasionally, three chapters and an outline of a young adult novel.

At the end of the semester, we had a tea and invited guests to view the student books. It was always an inspiring exhibit for anyone interested in producing their own book for children. All of the books were heartfelt and sparkled with originality. I remember particularly:

- *Fish Not Fish by Pam Crane with clever rhymes such as "You won't find it in a jungle where it's dark so why do they call it TIGER SHARK?!" The brightly colored illustration by Harold Peterson showed the reader why.*

- *I can dress by Alissa Andrews was a cloth book with real zippers and belts, buttons and bows, a small child's hands-on delight.*

- *I Know I Can was created by a teacher: a can filled with posters and velcro numbers, letters, and pictures to attach in appropriate places.*

- *Pots and Pans and Little Hands was Letha Berna's cookbook of easy culinary delights for children.*

- *What's the Word by Fred Plunkett, an engaging picture book about resisting drugs (no is the word) had a moving dedication: To my brother Farrell, and all the rest of the children in the world, for they are the future.*

My favorite of all times would have done world-renowned folklorists Peter and Iona Opie proud:

- *Rhymes and Times 1991 by Pat Jolly who visited five schools (public, private and parochial) and collected ninety-five playground rhymes, illustrated by the children themselves. The fascinating, scholarly result demonstrates how children see themselves and how diverse cultures (Afro-American, Hispanic, Vietnamese) melt together in the universality of childhood.*

Anyone searching for clues as to what makes a book children will love for more than a decade should follow Pat Jolly's example and listen when children play!

you when you try to create your own book for children. You will see where you fit into the complex, ever-changing marketplace. You will see where your talents and interests lie, which is where you should be if you want to get published. But don't forget as you study the categories that they overlap, and don't let the idea of categories inhibit you.

Here then are the main categories by genre with all you ever wanted to know about each, or at least, with everything we can think of that might help you. Please keep in mind everything we've said about books that defy categorizing and the overlapping of genres.

FICTION

PICTURE BOOKS

Definition:
A book for very young children in which the illustrations play at least as important a role as the text and sometimes carry part of the plot.

Age Level:
Preschool and kindergarten to second grade

Examples:
Where the Wild Things Are by Maurice Sendak: Max, a naughty boy is sent to his room where he travels in his imagination to the land ruled by monsters (his emotions). If you read this story without looking at the illustrations it would not make sense. Compare this to *The Tale of Peter Rabbit* by Beatrix Potter and you will see that *Peter is* an "illustrated book" not a "picture book" because it can be read without looking at the illustrations.

Goodnight Moon by Margaret Wise

"Call me shallow—I like 'Goodnight Moon.'"

Brown is a bedtime story meant to be read aloud (until the child learns it by heart!). Clement Hurd's illustrations are needed for an understanding of the text; they portray the necessary details and add to the tranquil mood of this small classic.

Millions of Cats by Wanda Gàg was published in 1928 and was the first true picture book ever if you accept the definition that the illustrations are at least as important to the whole as the text. Gàg's cursive text is part of the illustrations; together they make each page an art form. Beloved by children, it has never gone out of print and is a marvelous book for the student of picture books to dissect and study.

A   Ape.   a

B   Bear.   b

The Market:

As our book goes to press in 1997, the picture book is the most crowded category in all of children's books, and the most difficult to break into. However, it goes without saying that if you have a wonderful idea and this is the area you want to work in, there is always room for one more great book.

Skills Needed:

Include a childlike point of view, a love of language, the mind of a poet and one simple, strong idea. It needn't be something new, but your approach or angle has to be fresh. For example, there are dozens of alphabet books published every year and there's almost always at least one winner, original and unique in concept and execution. Check your bookstore for the latest and best. Of course, if you are an illustrator, this is your primary category, but don't neglect other categories if you're not quite ready for strong competition from some of the best contemporary artists. And don't forget either that some of the best illustrators don't write, they retell old folk and fairy tales or the lyrics to songs (e.g., Peter Spier) all in the public domain and not copyrighted and use them as vehicles for their marvelous illustrations.

C   Cock.   c

D   Dog.   d

Case History

In an interview, Nancy Willard gave this definition of a picture book: "A picture book is really very close to a poem. Once I asked an editor for a definition of a picture book, and she said, 'Well, I'll tell you what it isn't. A picture book is not a very short story.' A picture book is as rhythmic as a poem and has a lot in common with a poem. In a poem you have a line break and a stanza break, and in a picture book, you have the page turn, but in either one you have that recurring silence and you have to remember it in your text. You can have a long, long line of poem. And in a picture book you can have so much text on a page before you can turn it. It's a poem that is meant to be heard. Parents will read the lines over and over to children, and children will memorize them."

WRITING AND ILLUSTRATING EXERCISE

This can be your project if you are using this book as a how-to text. All of the other exercises and checklists will relate to it if you want to complete a publishable manuscript as you work through this "course." Based on the information in this step, decide on a category you believe offers you the best opportunity to express your book idea. Now begin to write and/or illustrate your book and plan to send off your manuscript and/or dummy to a publisher. If you have chosen to create a picture book, make a dummy (hand-made book) and either illustrate it or have someone you know collaborate. (Your illustrator can be a child; children are less inhibited than most adults!) Most picture books have thirty-two pages plus a cover and end sheets, with a title and credit page and the text beginning on pages 4-5. Choose a size appropriate to your subject matter. If your book is accepted by a publisher, she will almost certainly change the specifications; the important thing now is to make the irresistible presentation already so clear in your mind!

If you are doing a chapter book for children roughly eight to ten, don't bother to illustrate unless illustration is your major interest. You should, however, think about what illustrations are needed if any. Make sure the text is as good as you can possibly make it, and indicate with a sketch any illustration that is needed for meaning.

If you are writing a YA novel, make an outline and complete three chapters to show an editor, but be prepared because if he is interested, he'll want to see the rest of the book.

Berthe's Tulane students claimed they started thinking about their books at the beginning of the semester and often neglected other assignments to create their books. Maybe some of them exaggerated, hoping to get better grades, but they all completed the assignment in less than twelve weeks.

You can write a picture book and make a book dummy in less than two weeks. Writing longer books can take years or a few months, but for your purposes, a short chapter book or three chapters and an outline can be done in eight to ten weeks.

Subcategories:

Many different kinds of picture books and genres overlap or don't fit neatly anywhere, such as interactive books, poetry, fantasy, to name a few. We will look at these categories later in the chapter.

CHAPTER BOOKS

Definition:

Slightly longer books with more advanced subject matter, often easy-to-read books for beginners just learning.

Age Level and Examples:

Six to eight years old

Example: *Frog and Toad Are Friends* by Arnold Lobel, who also drew the delightful illustrations, is for the youngest in this category. Notice especially the humor and story that entertain

as well as educate. Books shouldn't preach; good books do teach but in a way the reader doesn't know it's happening. If you want to write a sermon, become a preacher. If you want to show children something about the meaning of life, give them a good story and read Bruno Bettelheim's *The Uses of Enchantment*.

Charlotte's Web is in the chapter books category for an older age group.

The Market:

No market is begging these days and you'll be competing with best-selling series like *The Babysitters Club* and *Goosebumps*, but schools are still looking for good books for this age level. Try publishing houses like Scholastic and Houghton Mifflin who have strong school lines. And do a little research and find the smaller specialty publishing houses. It pays to know what each publisher publishes before you waste time sending the wrong book to the wrong publisher.

Skills Needed:

Experience with children is essential unless you are a second Maurice Sendak. Librarians, teachers, this may be your area; you know what children want and what they need and you know what's not in the library. Write it yourself!

Subcategories:

There is a great variety of subject matter to choose from in this area. Visit a school library and your children's bookseller and poke around, asking about what is popular and why. This is a great age for nonfiction and the market is eager too. Again you're competing with great series such as the Eyewitness Books.

THE YOUNG ADULT NOVEL
Definition:

There are two kinds of young adult (YA) novel, one for ten to twelve years old and the other, twelve and up, much more

---

CASE HISTORY

Beverly Cleary was a librarian and was constantly asked for a kind of book not on the shelves. The children wanted to read about other children like themselves, so she wrote Ramona *and the rest, as they say… An editor published her book without changing a word.*

WRITING EXERCISE

Nancy Willard also suggested an interesting exercise: "The entire text of Night Story *(a picture book by Nancy Willard) started out as a poem published in an anthology and someone said it would make a wonderful picture book and set it up that way so each line is a page with a picture. It is a particular form which I think is very useful if you are just starting to write for children and you want to know how to begin. It is in a form called a litany, which gives you enough structure so that you can choose something to get hold of but does not hamper you. It's not rhymed but every line starts with the same word. You hear litanies in church and the psalms are full of poems of that sort.* Goodnight Moon *is written this way. It is a very mysterious form but if you want to write a picture book text, start there because you have so much to go on."*

CASE HISTORY (BERTHE)

We came home to New Orleans from Europe, my husband and I with six children, ranging in age from one to sixteen. Mark, our happy, well-adjusted eight-year-old spoke three languages including English and could read Flemish, but his teacher in the third grade of a public school made him feel stupid because he couldn't read English. Enter Dr. Seuss books! I will never forget watching Mark read aloud One fish, two fish, red fish, blue fish. *When he had finished he looked up at me and shouted, "I can read!" I met Dr. Seuss many years later and couldn't wait to tell him Mark's story. There were at least four other people trying to tell him their own reading success stories!*

sophisticated and almost on a level with adult fiction.

Age Level & Examples:

A few years ago we would have said that all of Robert Cormier's books (*The Chocolate War*) and some of Richard Peck's (*Are You in the House Alone?*) belonged in the older group, but now it seems the two groups have almost merged and younger children are reading all of the YA's while the twelves and up are reading adult fiction.

The Market:

The borderline between the twelve-and-ups and adult fiction has blurred and it's a tough market. If there's any

category almost crying for good books it's the young YA, ages nine to eleven. Fantasy is in again so you don't have to worry about attacking contemporary social problems if that's not your forte. On the other hand, if you're an expert in any of the young adult problem fields, they need books there too.

NONFICTION

Nonfiction offers more possibilities than ever before for writers and illustrators of children's books. The school market has grown bigger for books beyond the old-fashioned kinds of textbooks that presented science and math in a dry way. Now books vie with each other to make school subjects more accessible and intriguing even to the picture book crowd. What kid, or what grown-up for that matter, is not fascinated by David M. Schwartz's comparisons and Steven Kellogg's incomparable illustrations in *How Much Is a Million?* ("If a goldfish bowl were big enough for a million goldfish, it would be large enough to hold a whale.") Each of the Eyewitness Books, a series covering almost every subject you can imagine (weather, sports, ancient Egypt) has a large format, and is factual with scanty text and tons of photos and illustrations, a visual feast of a textbook!

EXERCISE

Go to a children's bookstore or to a good school library and analyze at least half a dozen biographies that appeal to you. What approach has the author or illustrator taken that makes this a good book? Now find some biographies you think are boring and choose one to rework. How would you make it interesting? Rethinking other people's books will help you see your manuscript from a new point of view.

BIOGRAPHY, AUTOBIOGRAPHY AND (HERE WE GO AGAIN JUMPING CATEGORY BOUNDARIES) FICTIONALIZED BIOGRAPHY:

How the scene has changed! Again, it's the pressure to make relatively dry subjects more intriguing and accessible to young children that has opened up as never before this genre to writers and illustrators of picture books. Teachers and librarians rejoice in such books as Barbara Nichol's *Beethoven Lives Upstairs* for early readers, Diane Stanley's beautifully illustrated, well researched *Bard of Avon: The Story of William Shakespeare*, and prizewinning *Emily*, the fictionalized picture-book story of poet Emily Dickinson.

Note from the following short list of books that this genre encompasses a variety of interests and fits all ages:

Starry Messenger by Peter Sis is the story of Galileo.

Hiding to Survive by Maxine B. Rosenberg is a collection of stories about Jewish children rescued from the Holocaust.

Dominique Moceanu as told to Steve Woodward is the autobiography of an American champion.

CASE HISTORY (BERTHE)

Ursula Nordstrom once said to me, "Make every word count!" She was objecting to a cliché I'd used in my first YA manuscript, something like "his heart stood still." But I have since thought how much more that admonition applies to picture books and to poetry, both of which use few words.

It's strange how casually spoken words can sometimes take on lasting meaning and influence you. Be conscious of the power of words and listen for "magic words." When my husband and I were in our twenties just starting out, he once said, "If you aim for good you'll never get to best." He was talking about something that had nothing to do with either of us, but those were "magic words" for me and I remembered them when I was trying to get published.

I needed courage (or maybe it was nerve) in those days in the sixties. Mary Cable, a published, well-respected writer, gave me "magic words" when I was going to New York, alone, pregnant and terrified. She said, "Just barge right on in! They're (editors) looking for talent." The second part of her advice still holds true, but these days, you need an appointment!

MOTHER GOOSE.

Freedom's Children, Young Civil Rights Activists Tell Their Own Stories by Ellen Levine.

The Diary of Anne Frank is still the classic trendsetter in this genre.

Invincible Louisa by Cornelia Meigs, the biography of Louisa May Alcott, won the Newbery in 1933 and is still in print.

If you analyze these books with the idea this is the genre for you, look for the qualities that make these books stand out in the crowd: interesting subject, good writing and illustration, an unusual or original point of view. In Step 8, Rethinking Your Story, is Whitney Stewart's case history, good reading for anyone interested in writing biographies.

Beth Woods
Education 614
Professor Amoss
October 6, 1993

Children's Rhymes

I won't go to Macy's no more no more.

There's a big fat policeman by the door door door.

He grabbed me by the collar, and he made me pay a dollar,

So I won't go to Macy's no more no more.

POETRY

Poetry is wonderful if you're a poet and to be avoided like the plague if you're not. Don't be fooled into thinking that imitating Dr. Seuss is the way to go. Dr. Seuss was a genius, a Renaissance man living in our times and in children's literature. He had a magical understanding of children and spoke their secret language.

It's a mistake to think that doggerel verse is a key to success with children; nothing turns an editor off more quickly than the couplet that ends with a word that almost fits.

So much for those of us who are not poets! For those who are, poetry is a hard sell at best. The truth is that most editors publish very little poetry and usually rely on a few contemporary big names or the old tried-and-true classics and Mother Goose rhymes.

Having said all of those discouraging words, we will address the survival of the fittest, those of you who love and want to write poetry or those of you who are absolutely positive that your story should be in verse. Poetry speaks to the child as nothing else does. By its nature, it sings and the child sings with it or it comforts and the child is content. Poetry feeds the imagination; poetry never scolds and never lectures, although like all good literature it helps a child find meaning in her world.

And so if poetry is what you love, that is where you belong. Read as much of it as you can lay your hands on, especially books being published now. Here is a brief list of popular books that are either straight poetry or use poetry as an important part of the text:

Classics:

Nonsense Songs and Stories by Edward Lear. Amusing line drawings, made-up words and musical rhymes keep this early nineteenth-century collection as funny and pleasing to children now as then.

A Child's Garden of Verses by Robert Louis Stevenson. Published in 1885 and still in print in many editions.

The Oxford Dictionary of Nursery Rhymes edited by Iona and Peter

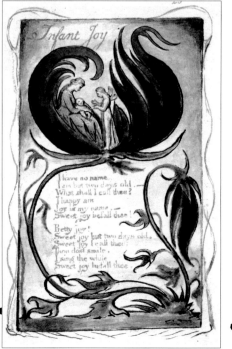

WRITING EXERCISE

Check out from your library a good anthology of poetry for children and see how many qualities the poems have in common (rhythmic repetition, onomatopoeia, rhyming, refrains, etc.).

Opie. There are hundreds of excellent collections of traditional nursery rhymes and Mother Goose rhymes, but the Opies' edition is annotated with old woodcut and nineteenth-century illustrations and is one of the best. Nursery rhymes and classic fairy tales are in the public domain, which means writers and illustrators can use them without obtaining permission from anyone.

Songs of Innocence and Experience by William Blake. This book was the inspiration for Nancy Willard's Newbery Medal winner, *A Visit to William Blake's Inn*, the first book of poetry ever to win this prestigious award.

Other poets who speak to children and are still heard by them: Emily Dickinson, Walt Whitman, Eugene Field, Edgar Allan Poe, Rudyard Kipling, William Wordsworth, Lewis Carroll and A.A. Milne.

Look for clues to child appeal in the works of these old favorites. You can get a sampling from each in a good anthology such as the popular *Sing a Song of Popcorn*, edited by Beatrice Schenk de Regniers.

More recent poets who have won the hearts of young readers and are therefore worth your while to study include Randall Jarrell, Nancy Willard, Eve Merriam, and in a class all to themselves Shel Silverstein (*A Light in the Attic*) and Jack Prelutsky (*A Pizza the Size of the Sun* illustrated by James Stevenson).

FANTASY AND SCIENCE FICTION

Both fantasy and science fiction are terrifically popular genres if you have the knack and love them yourself. We've lumped them together because they are not of this world, but actually, you may love one and not the other because there's a difference: fantasy tends to deal in unreality in dragons, magicians, fairies, the battle between good and evil in an enchanted world. Science

fiction is more realistic and is based more on futuristic concepts and surreal, remote possibilities.

This is the land of series and sequels, trilogies and monopolies. You'll have to create your own kingdom or future world and compete with masters, William Sleator (*Oddballs*) for your science fiction title and with Robin McKinley (*The Hero and the Crown*) for fantasy. But never mind, you'll find their books are entertaining and have surprising depths.

George MacDonald (*The Princess and Curdie*) was one of the earliest, great fantasists and the role model for C.S. Lewis and his Narnia books. Read Lloyd Alexander and Susan Cooper for contemporary masters of fantasy.

The Market:
If you have the talent, this is the place for you. There are a lot of titles out there already and several formidable series that children devour, but if fantasy or science fiction is your love, go for it.

CASE HISTORY

Nancy Willard told this story: "There is no good children's book that is only for children. The kind of literature that crosses the boundary most often between adult and children is fantasy, which is really for all ages. One of my favorite books of fantasy is Alice in Wonderland. *I read it when I was eight and I was much amused to hear a friend say that he had to go into the hospital for an eye operation and was allowed to read for only one hour a day for an extended period of time. What book could he bring that would sustain him? He didn't bring the Bible because I think he already knew it so well. He wanted something that would make him laugh and keep up his interest for that precious hour. He brought* Alice in Wonderland. *You can call it a book for children, but clearly, it's a book for all ages.*

I think that is also true of fairy tales. Fairy tales were originally told by grown-ups to other grown-ups, by women to other women as they sat in their spinning rooms in their houses passing time."

WORDLESS BOOKS

If you're an illustrator this might seem a category just made for you and maybe it is. But what you'll need in addition to artistic talent is a particularly good sense of story because your illustrations will have to carry the whole book, plot and all, without the help of words.

Lynd Ward was more illustrator than writer. When he wrote his beloved *The Biggest Bear*, he did all of the illustrations (large, monochrome oils) first and hung them up on the wall. Then, he walked from painting to painting and wrote the words.

When David Wiesner won the Caldecott Medal for his wordless book *Tuesday*, he was already an accomplished, recognized book illustrator with a string of honors in his wake. *Tuesday* is a wild stretch of the imagination with weird, mysterious, gorgeous illustrations done from the perspective of frogs! It is a wonderful wordless book to enjoy and study.

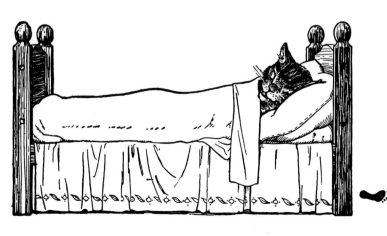

INTERACTIVE OR BOOKS PLUS

Every major publisher has a batch of interactive books, ranging from simple lift-the-flap books to books so loaded down with objects for children to play with that the actual book and reading is relegated to second place. One company whose products are sold in bookstores started out attaching little sacks of objects to the book cover and now has their own huge display stand of so-called books with everything from sand toys to hair ribbons. If you love clever design, paper engineering, all of the wonderfully creative things that belong to this genre, this is the category for you to explore and no better place than in the bookstore at Christmastime.

Small children love books that do things. Interactive books are a great way to let children know that good things happen between the pages of a book, and a clever, simple gimmick will get the attention of an editor. But keep it very simple; if your idea is too complicated, it means production difficulties and expense, things no publisher is willing to tackle if you are unknown.

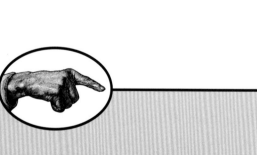

CHECKLIST

Before you send your manuscript off, make sure you know who your audience is. It is a common mistake, sometimes even made by publishers, to present a sophisticated subject in a format designed for very young children – a well-known book leaps to mind: The story of the bomb dropped on Hiroshima in a picture book format! If you want to teach small children that war is terrible, begin with a conflict within their experience and show them that kicking the dog is wrong. A child's book must not go beyond the level of a child's experience.

Studying the categories of children's books is a fascinating, ongoing experience, a giant step on your way to publishing your own book.

STEP 3

Finding Your Audience

Remember the old joke about how you get to Carnegie Hall? Practice, practice. Well, the same is true for children's books. The aspiring violinist or opera singer wants to reach an audience – the best audience for his kind of music, a Carnegie Hall audience. To reach that audience, the musician must impress other audiences along the way. Parents or teachers who will encourage or pay for further training; better and better teachers to help hone skills; impresarios or conductors; agents; and finally, the soloist gets a Carnegie Hall debut.

You must be willing to demonstrate similar persistence if you hope to succeed as a children's-book author or illustrator. As you strive to hone your skills with patience and dedication, it helps to seek out the best influences. If you have the native talent and drive to succeed, you will attract the attention of these individuals. But keep singing your merits until you reach a stage where you can finally face your ideal audience.

Recognize that, like the aspiring musician, you have many audiences to conquer before you get to the main stage. First, you must have the native talent to attract the encouragement of discerning individuals. Frequently, such talent will manifest itself while you are still a child. If you do not have parents

SOMEDAY YOU'LL THANK ME!

EINE KLEINE NACHT MUSIK

CASE HISTORY (BERTHE)

I remember hearing Charlotte Zolotow (legendary author of more than sixty picture books) say, "I've had an idea for a picture book for two years, but I can't make it work yet." I had an idea for a T-shirt illustration for two days. Linda Armantrout and I were manning a booth at ABA, and our neighbor had music books. He suggested a musical theme for a T-shirt, and I came up with Mozart practicing the piano and his mother standing over him. But Linda and I couldn't think of the words that would work. One day Linda shouted, "Someday you'll thank me!" and a winner was born.

CASE HISTORY (ERIC)

I can still recall what my third-grade teacher wrote on my final report card for the year: "Eric has all the earmarks of a fine writer." At the time, I had no idea what "earmarks" were. But these words stayed with me from that time to this. After third grade, I sought out opportunities to write- – was an editor of my junior high school newspaper, editor-in-chief of my high school newspaper; chief theater critic of my college newspaper; theater editor of the The Villager *newspaper. When I was an editorial assistant at Golden Books, I proposed book projects to the senior editors so that I would be asked to do the writing. My first byline in a book was in* The Elves and the Shoemaker, *a Little Golden Book that went through several editions. It all starts with a pat on the back in third grade. My first audience was wonderful Mrs. Beasing at P.S. 2!*

predisposed to recognize creative talent, a teacher may have singled you out. Sometimes such talent does not show itself until later. But as Beverly Sills once said of becoming an opera singer, both native talent and good training are required.

As an opera singer develops her voice, so you must develop your talent and work up a set of skills, or a technique. You may be full of good ideas, but until you know you can communicate them effectively at any time, you cannot confidently launch yourself on a career as a writer for children. First, you need training. We tend to undervalue writing because it is something each of us is taught to do in school. We all think we have the basic skills. But writing for a special audience requires special skills, and you will not get to play Carnegie Hall – get published by Random House! – without the ability to project to those listeners.

Writing a children's book is different from writing a term paper, or a newspaper article, or an office memo. Children's books have their own conventions, which may vary by format and age group. Think of it this way – all fairy tales begin with the words "Once upon a time" and end with the reassuring thought that "They lived happily ever after." It helps to understand that fairy tales grow out of an oral tradition, as did Homer's epics. The stock phrases were part of that tradition, helping the audience achieve a level of comfort with a story that would have been more strange and

difficult without the conventions. As any student of the Grimms knows, anything can happen between the stock opening and the stock ending, but those conventions help frame the story and let the listener know when the story is beginning and when it is ending – important indeed if you are sitting wide-eyed in a dark hut in the Black Forest, or if you are a child waiting for or trying to avoid the moment of truth – bedtime!

This is not to suggest you will be writing fairy tales. You will be writing your story, but in a form recognizable as a children's book. The main requirement is that your story must be comprehensible at the level of a child's experience, and you need to have a childlike point of view. To get to a point where you can learn how to write in this form without thinking about it, it might help you to take classes and attend workshops. These possibilities are

explored in detail in Step 6. And, of course, you need to read as many children's books as you can, and you need to write, write, write.

The formalities of children's books have broken down in the last fifty years. Margaret Wise Brown, with her free-form nonstories (*Goodnight Moon*); Maurice Sendak, with wordless pages conveying the important emotions of the story (*Where the Wild Things Are*); Chris Van Allsburg, with his enigmatic episodes (*Jumanji*) – all have broken down the idea of the picture book as a story with a beginning, middle and end. Brown, Sendak and Van Allsburg are geniuses, but even they had to master the rudiments of plotting a book before they could do their most distinctive work. Sendak illustrated the work of other writers – some of the best in the business – for years before writing and illustrating *Where the Wild Things Are*. He learned at the feet of masters and was also a student of German fairy tales and illustrations.

WRITING EXERCISE

Go to the library and check out Brown's books and those of other authors mentioned on this page. Analyze them, looking for the following elements and the uses to which they are put:

- *repetition*
- *absence of words or pictures on a page*
- *assonance, or repetition of similar sounds ("frail as air")*
- *dissonance, or use of contrasting sounds ("dark gray river/soft white snow"); alliteration, or use of words with similar beginning sounds ("four fur feet")*
- *rhyme, including internal rhyme ("It would have seemed very funny not to be a Bunny.")*
- *theme, subject matter, message*

Even if there is no plot as such, you should look for the elements that give the story logic and make it work.

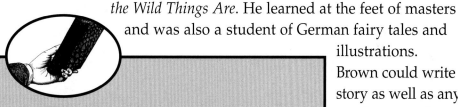

CASE HISTORY (ERIC)

One of the thrills of my career was publishing a posthumous work by Margaret Wise Brown. My boss learned that Brown had left her papers to a small public library in Westerly, Rhode Island. I was duly dispatched to pore over this treasure trove. I drove to Westerly and was left alone in a room containing one tantalizing steel file cabinet. What I found inside was mostly disappointing – preliminary, not-as-good drafts of many of Brown's well-known works, modern "adult" poetry–but there were a couple of gems. One was called "Birthdays in the Woods." I immediately saw it as a companion to her classics The Golden Egg Book *and* The Golden Bunny. *To show that innovation remains challenging even years after the event, my boss hated the manuscript and so did her successor. Once I succeeded to the top editorial spot, I was able to push the project as a publishing "event." One last hurdle–the approval of Brown's estate was conditional on our using only an illustrator who had worked with Brown during her lifetime and who would be familiar with her creative process. What a blessing that Leonard Weisgard was available to do the honors!*

Brown could write a story as well as anyone; but even her boldest inventions are intricate progressions that gain suspense from patterns of language and event. Indeed, Brown was affiliated with the well-known Bank Street Laboratory, whose members produced some of the most distinctive children's books of the postwar years. Moreover, Brown frequently collaborated with other Bank Street writers – Edith Thacher Hurd, for instance. When writing under her own byline or pseudonym, Brown always collaborated closely with illustrators – Leonard Weisgard, Garth Williams, Remy Charlip – who were masters of format and form and could express Brown's perfectly controlled sequences, allowing her the freedom to play with the words.

EXERCISE

Visualize your ideal audience in your mind's eye. Now think about the book that would make that reader scream for more. Think about the feature that works the magic. Is it a pop-up or other interactive feature? If your ideal reader is older, is the "scream feature" a cliff-hanger ending to every chapter? Draw a line down the center of a piece of paper. On the left-hand side, write down five ideas for stories. In the right-hand column, write the feature that would enhance such a story's appeal.

The skills you need to develop may vary by the type of children's book you want to write. If you want to write picture books for toddlers, you must master certain formats and the ability to write very, very simply. If you want to write novels for teenagers, you may need to immerse yourself in a different kind of literature and set of concerns. To some extent, these decisions will be made for you by your own particular interests. But many writers at the beginning have tried to cram too much story into a picture book, or spread a basically simple tale into a full-length novel. Know your limits, as well as the boundaries of the available formats. Step 2 in this book should have helped you understand these categories.

Even if you have a clear sense of the type of books you want to write or children you want to reach,

CASE HISTORY

*Beatrix Potter got started on her publishing career because she had struck up a correspondence with a small child. Her letters were filled with little stories and decorated with exquisite watercolors. From writing to one child, she conquered the world! Kenneth Grahame (*The Wind in the Willows*), A.A. Milne (*Winnie-the-Pooh*) and Edward Ardizzone (the* Lucy and Tim *books) were loving fathers who wrote some of their great stories specifically for their own children. Lewis Carroll wrote* Alice in Wonderland *for and about a real little girl who was the daughter of friends. But you don't need to have a specific child in mind to write successfully. If you are one of the lucky few with a lively "child within" (the ability to see the world as a child does), you will not need to consult any other "audience."*

your audience for a children's book is not an easy one to pinpoint. That is because you have several audiences. First are editors, then booksellers. Then come parents and educators. And only then come the children. How can you appeal to all these audiences?

First, you can appeal to editors by targeting ones who seem to like the kind of book you are writing. How do you know this? Through research, networking, talking to your published friends. You can also find clues in the books they have published. Go on the Internet and chat to others in the field. Go to writer's conferences or classes where editors are the guest speakers. If there is an opportunity to have your manuscript read by an editor, go for it. Seek out local teachers of writing for children – chances are they will have some contacts in the publishing world. Librarians and booksellers may also have such contacts.

In many ways, educators and librarians are the most influential audience. They are the powers behind most of the critical press and awards committees in the children's-book arena. They also control the purse strings when it comes to purchasing quantities of new books for classroom and library use. Nevertheless, as you will see in Step 7, truly distinctive markets for books may be a thing of the past. Today's parents, albeit less critical than educators, are the force to be reckoned with in children's-book sales.

How do you appeal to parents? By putting elements that parents like into your book. The creators of *Sesame Street* were expert at putting in humor and jokes that parents would get though their children might not. Think about the books you would like your children to have. You want your children to like reading, so you want the books to be entertaining and readable. But you also want your children to learn something from their books – about numbers, or a historical period, or freedom. If you are writing nonfiction books, it's easy to make your writing teach something. However,

CASE HISTORY (ERIC)

Cyndy Szekeres, the wonderful illustrator of fuzzy animals, long wanted to do a book about hugs but there was never really time because she was always doing new books that were more complex and told stories. One day, I was looking through Cyndy's books and realized that many, if not all, featured hugs at some point. We were able to cull these pictures from the different books and put them together in a little board book called Hugs, *with Cyndy's rhyming text. But even this very simple book had a plot–the hugs were arranged in a "through the day" pattern, ending with suppertime, bathtime and bedtime. This allowed the toddler to "see" his own experience again, reflected in the pages of a book. Perfect for tiny readers, and one of* Publishers Weekly's *best-sellers for that year.*

this challenge becomes more difficult when you write fiction. You don't want your stories to become didactic, so you have to make the teaching a convincing part of your entertaining story. Creative authors and illustrators have found lots of great solutions to this dilemma. A book like *The Five Chinese Brothers*, by Claire H. Bishop and Kurt Wiese, is a perfect example of an entertaining story that illustrates a strong theme about being part of a family but still being an individual. And the reinforcement of the concept of "five" is a great bonus!

As much as you want parents to approve of and like (and buy!) your book, don't pander to parents at the expense of children's interests. Many classics feed a child's growing sense of independence, and this in turn fuels the child's psychological development and progress toward adulthood. In *The Uses of Enchantment*, psychologist Bruno Bettelheim describes how some of the most popular fairy tales subtly reflect the child's growth away from parents into a self-sufficient adulthood. Books can show how children begin to turn away from parents, and some parents may find these books disturbing. Remember that some books parents dislike – like some of Judy Blume's young adult novels – become best-sellers nevertheless.

Most importantly, how do you appeal to children? Here is the paradox in finding your audience: Your writing must appeal to editors and parents – adults, in short – but you must always be writing with children in mind. In a real sense, this is the audience your writing is "for," and you must never lose sight of that fact. But children are not a monolithic group – there are many subcategories of children, and you should think carefully about how you classify your audience. Be as specific as you can. Frequently, the desire to communicate with a specific child is the springboard for creativity.

Think about the vast range of children's books from the point of view of readers' ages. Some books are for tiny "readers" who cannot yet even recognize letters. Some are for teenagers who can read sophisticated novels and nonfiction books to themselves. And there is a tremendous number in between.

How can you, the writer, master this information? Keep it simple. It is a logical progression. The books for babies who cannot yet read

CASE HISTORY (ERIC)

A young lawyer and her husband were caring for a small nephew who had trouble getting started in the morning. The lawyer developed a little saying to speed the child along – "Quickly, Quigley." One day, the child asked who was Quigley. The aunt made up a story about a slowpoke penguin. She liked the story and wrote it down. Quickly Quigley *found publishers in England and the United States and was the first published book by Jeanne Gravois! The desire to communicate with a specific child led to the creation of a book with wide appeal.*

EXERCISE

Try to glean writer's guidelines for your chosen age group by analyzing successful stories for that age reader. In the example of Three Billy Goats Gruff, *you learn the importance of repetition, of a simple but satisfying resolution, of creating a vehicle for comprehensible pictures, and of identifying a story that can be told in few and simple words, including catchy dialogue children can enjoy repeating. These are features of books for children aged two to five. Later, as children develop more sense of cause and effect, your stories can become less circular and more linear, with less repetition and more character development.*

will be very basic. Usually they will not even tell a story as such but just be a sequence of pictures organized around some theme or basic idea.

Think about how we grow and how our ideas evolve. Babies and very young children love to play peekaboo. The excitement comes from not knowing whether the thing or person who disappears will ever come back. This is where our passion for suspense begins. Here, too, is the beginning of story – a quest for something that may never be found. In *Three Billy Goats Gruff*, we wonder whether the goats will ever see the other side of the bridge. In *Outside Over There*, we wonder whether the heroine will see her baby sister again. In *The Incredible Journey*, we wonder whether the animals will find their human family. In *Gone With the Wind*, we wonder whether Scarlett will return to Tara. From babyhood to adulthood, all using the simple idea of peekaboo.

But how do you develop this idea and target the reader you want to reach? First, look back to your ideal audience. Is it a little child who would be tantalized by the goats' predicament? If so, think about the goats' story and what it teaches you about successful storytelling for the very young. Repetition is very important – in fact, the plot basically recounts the same episode three times with minor variations until a resolution is achieved. The plot can be told in very few words and has a simplicity that lends itself to bold, entertaining pictures. There is just enough variety to make the pictures interesting by virtue of the different sizes of the goats and the different ending to the story's third and final episode.

Picture books are the genre of choice for children up to about seven years old. As the target audience becomes older, the stories can become more sophisticated and delve deeper into the characters and reasons for things.

CASE HISTORY (ERIC)

Publishers usually acquire manuscripts for their beginning reader series by sending their technical guidelines to experienced writers in the genre. Sometimes, however, a story comes in that is told in few words and features frequent repetition and so suggests itself as a beginning reader. I once received a submission from the wonderful writer Jan Wahl. The story, entitled Rabbits on Roller Skates, *was essentially a series of tableaux of rabbits roller skating uphill, downhill, etc. It didn't seem like much of a story to me, and I rejected it. An editor at Crown saw in it a potential entry for that publisher's "easy-to-read" line, and the book was published to some acclaim.*

WRITING EXERCISE

Think about children you know. What are their ages? What are their interests? Write the first sentence of a story that would interest each of them. Be conscious of varying language by age group. Could the same story interest children of different ages and abilities if told with different words and emphasis?

However, this is not a license to use more words! Maurice Sendak's *Outside Over There* and several of Chris Van Allsburg's books demonstrate how picture books can be sophisticated, even "deep," without excess verbiage. The trick is in the pictures!

At around age six or seven children begin to read for themselves and need books that entertain them while reinforcing their reading skills. There are numerous series of books in the vein of the "I Can Read" line published by HarperCollins, which features controlled vocabulary, high-interest subject matter and a system coded to reflect different levels of reading skill.

Publishers often employ complex and technical methods to determine appropriate vocabulary lists, word repetitions and word counts for early readers of differing abilities. Unless you have demonstrable expertise in reading pedagogy, you may not find many opportunities to write stories in this format.

However, there is room for imaginative, individualistic writing in this age group. Think about Dr. Seuss (*The Cat in the Hat*), Else Holmlund Minarik (the Little Bear books), Arnold Lobel (the Frog and Toad series). The trick is to write stories sophisticated enough to entertain older children but told in language simple enough for them to read to themselves. Paradoxically, the language in books for these older children must often be simpler than that found in picture books for their younger siblings! With picture books, it is parents and other adults who do the actual reading.

Children rapidly outgrow "easy-to-read" books and want more substantial fare. Chapter books are the next step in children's progress to adult reading. Books like *Homer Price*, the Encyclopedia Brown stories, and Beverly Cleary's novels (e.g., *Henry and Beezus*) are good examples of entertaining stories told in strong, simple prose and subdivided into manageable chunks for children to read and digest. After this stage, children enter the realm of the "young adult" books that are close to adult in language and theme but feature preteen or teenage characters.

In addition to targeting specific

CASE HISTORY (ERIC)

A literary agent was representing a new Latin American writer whose book told the story of a family living under politically repressive conditions in Central America. Due to the seriousness of the theme and the salability of Latin American fiction at the time, the agent sent the manuscript to editors of adult lists at major trade houses like Doubleday. No one took the book. Then the agent took a cue from the young age of the book's heroine, and started sending the manuscript to editors of young adult books. The book, The Honorable Prison *by Lyll Becerra de Jenkins, was published to acclaim and won the Scott O'Dell Award for historical fiction.*

READING LIST

The books on this list tell similar stories for very different audiences. Read the paired books and compare and contrast:

- Beauty and the Beast *by Marianna Mayer*
- Beauty *by Robin McKinley*

- The Biggest Bear *by Lynd Ward*
- The Yearling *by Marjorie Kinnan Rawlings*

- Noah's Ark *by Peter Spier*
- Many Waters *by Madeleine L'Engle*

- The Tale of Peter Rabbit *by Beatrix Potter*
- Rabbit Hill *by Robert Lawson*

age readers, writers may target children with other characteristics as well. While it is true a good story will speak to a wide range of readers, there has been some focus in recent years on providing children with a "multicultural" reading experience. This means that the books should reflect experiences beyond or different from those of white, Christian Americans. Books based on or about Asian-, African-, Latin- and Native Americans have been sought after by publishers. It used to be the accepted wisdom that white parents would not buy books with children of different ethnicities on the covers (and sales figures often sadly bore this out). However, with support from teachers and librarians eager to vary and supplement their curriculum materials, these books may now find wider audiences.

How can you target minority or other highly specific audiences? The simple

CASE HISTORY (ERIC)

At Golden Books, we published a book entitled Moving Day *that told the story of two young girls who were best friends. They were saddened when one of the girls had to move away, but learned their friendship could continue despite the physical distance between them. One little girl was white, one was African-American. In the original manuscript, the second girl was actually African and had a name with many vowels that could be difficult to pronounce. The editor asked the author to make the girl African-American and to simplify her name. The author complied. After the book was published and had disappointing sales, the marketing executives (who lived and worked in Racine, Wisconsin) decided the reason the book had failed was that the cover showed the two girls playing together. "Nobody sees black and white children playing together," they told us, so the cover should be changed. Living in a very mixed Manhattan neighborhood, I totally disagreed. But there was a lesson for the author in all this – Golden Books was not the right house for her story!*

answer is like the answer to how you write a young adult novel – by writing about characters who share characteristics with the audience you want to reach. This seems simple enough until you remember a few home truths. All publishers do not feel equally comfortable with publishing for minority readerships. Some publishers may resist your efforts to write about African-American characters, for instance, unless you yourself are African-American. And all minority experiences are not created equal – a book about white children in the South will not be perceived as "multicultural" but as "regional," giving publishers a reason to resist publishing.

It is also true a good story will reach its audience no matter how "different" the characters may seem. The children's stories of Isaac Bashevis Singer are classics, despite – or perhaps because of – the fact they depict Eastern European Jews living in shtetls, a world that no longer exists as a result of the Holocaust. Virginia Hamilton's novels (e.g., *M.C. Higgins, the Great*) continue to win accolades and be read everywhere, even by children who are not African-American. The only lesson for the writer is to understand that writing for a perceived "special" audience may engender some up-front resistance from publishers, and may mean the writer must do more research to identify publishers who will be receptive to the story featuring minority characters or concerns.

As always, spend time in bookstores looking for publishers who publish books like the one you want to write. Carefully note the publishers' names. And submit to those publishers on your list. Your targeted publishers are the best vehicle to help you find your target audience!

CHECKLIST

Think about all the audiences to whom you must appeal in getting your manuscript published. Review your manuscript and write down the elements you've included to appeal to each of these audiences.

Children:
- *Age of your ideal reader*
- *Format of your book*
- *Special characteristics of your ideal reader*

Parents:
- *Humor*
- *"Values"*
- *Educational content*

Editors:
- *Appropriateness of target audience and format*
- *High-interest (salable) subject matter*
- *"Special" features that may require special handling*

STEP 4

Seeing the Book as an Art Form

Y ou've now taken the first three steps and should have a clear sense of the type of book you want to write and what audience you want to reach. In this fourth step, we'll discuss the children's book as an art form to sharpen your sense of the type of book you want to write.

Books are an art form. With or without illustrations, books can be pleasing to the eye, and the content can move the reader in some profound way. Especially with children, a book can exert a powerful, developmental influence. In *The Uses of Enchantment*, Bruno Bettelheim wrote that potentially, books rank third after parents and educators in helping children find meaning in life.

Authors, illustrators and editors almost always think of their books as works of art. Great care is taken with the format, the quality of the paper, the typeface, the binding, cover and jacket, and the illustrations if any. Of course, the aesthetics have to be balanced with cost and marketing opportunities, but there is something about a book that has always attracted people who care about art. Most fine artists at one time or another try their hand at a one-of-a-kind book, as art for art's sake, and book lovers (your authors included) are among the most avid of collectors.

If you are creating a book, seeing it as an art form and understanding the possibilities of what can go into it are important steps toward a successful presentation to a publisher.

In this chapter, we will examine three very different

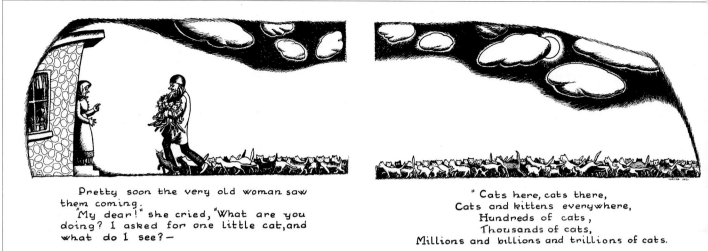

Pretty soon the very old woman saw them coming.
"My dear!" she cried, "What are you doing? I asked for one little cat, and what do I see? —

" Cats here, cats there,
Cats and kittens everywhere,
Hundreds of cats,
Thousands of cats,
Millions and billions and trillions of cats.

books as art forms: *Millions of Cats* by Wanda Gàg, *The Animal Family* by Randall Jarrell and "decorated" by Maurice Sendak, and *Pish, Posh, Said Hieronymous Bosch* by Nancy Willard, illustrated by Leo and Diane Dillon.

Millions of Cats, written and illustrated by Wanda *Gàg* in 1928, is considered the first true American picture book, if you accept our definition that the illustrations play as important a role as the text in the book as a whole.

We can learn almost all we have to know about picture books from this simple little story with its black-and-white illustrations. We recommend you either buy an inexpensive copy or check one out from your library.

WRITING AND ILLUSTRATING EXERCISE FOR *MILLIONS OF CATS* BY WANDA GÀG

Notice how the text is "hand-written." How would the page look if Gàg had used a typeface? Find a double spread (an illustration that stretches across two pages). How does this help the flow of the story? It is said that when her books were being printed, Gàg supervised and insisted that the black must be black and not a faded, dark dark gray! How does she keep her illustrations from crying out for color? Compare an old fairy tale in its original form (not adapted or changed, but translated) and notice the following characteristics shared by Millions of Cats: *no particular time, no specific place, no characterization, all information needed in first paragraph. Look at the illustrations in an early nineteenth-century book and notice the similarities: no color, simple, usually narrative as well as decorative. To appreciate fully the artistry of* Millions of Cats, *try imagining this book in full color with typeset and an embellished text (adjectives, adverbs and descriptions). For more insight into illustration and love of language, look for* Tales from Grimm, *lovingly translated from the German and illustrated by Wanda Gàg.*

Wanda Gàg was born in the closely knit, culturally German community of Ulm, Minnesota, around the turn of the century. Her father, a painter, and her sickly mother both died when Gàg, the oldest of five children, was still a teenager. She refused the kind offers of several families to take the children into their homes, and kept her siblings together, supporting them by doing odd jobs such as painting lampshades. She saw to it that they all received an education, which included familiarity with her beloved Grimm's fairy tales. Later, Gàg lived with a family as the nanny to their children and entertained them with her own stories and drawings. She became a recognized artist, a printmaker at a time when printmaking was having a renaissance and publishers were just beginning to see a need for more children's books. When an editor saw Wanda's work in a gallery show and asked her to produce a picture book, she had already written and illustrated *Millions of Cats* for the family of children she had lived with. It was published and was an instant success.

Millions of Cats is a picture book of thirty-two pages, with the illustrations carrying part of the plot and integral to the text. The text, in Gàg's cursive writing, is really a part of her page composition along with her black-and-white, woodcut-like drawings, neatly composed on the page. The illustrations flow between the pages, carrying the eye from page to page. Each page is carefully composed as a whole composition or two pages form a double spread (at that time, a new concept in books for children), one that takes the eye over the "gutter" (the separation made by the seam where the two pages meet) and joins the two pages in a complete picture.

The story is about a lonely, old couple who are looking for a little cat to keep them company. The simple plot takes the little old man on a walk to find the perfect cat. He finds millions of cats and they fight over which is prettiest until only one scrawny little cat is left.

In the illustrations we see the cat grow fatter and cuter until it becomes pretty and cuddly. There is the enticing refrain: "Cats here, cats there, cats and kittens everywhere, Hundreds of cats Thousands of cats, millions and billions and trillions of cats." And that is it: a very simple idea, cozy little black-and-white drawings, and pages that make a whole art object. The text is like a poem that is part of the illustration, and a story that is original and new in the same format as the old folk-fairy tales the brothers Grimm collected from storytellers in the early nineteenth century.

THE  HUNTER

The Animal Family by Randall Jarrell was not illustrated but rather "decorated" by Maurice Sendak. This is a remarkable collaboration of artists, both of whom loved the old fairy tales – not just the stories but the language and German culture of the early nineteenth century. They agreed that the text should not be illustrated; the reader could better imagine the images from the text. Sendak's ink drawings are all of inanimate objects. The theme of the book is the warmth of family and everything about the book contributes to establishing a feeling of contentment and security. The poetic text is like a happy dream, part fantasy, part ideal realism, and is surrounded by wide borders that seem

to hold the words as the walls of a small, cozy house might hold a family. The story itself is not sentimental but it is comforting, unassuming and full of wisdom, the beautiful vision of a poet, which Jarrell was. The paper is a fine quality and the type elegant yet simple. The size of the book is small and the shape a square. It is the kind of book you give to someone you love, and it is the kind of book that demonstrates a book without real illustrations can still be a work of art. This book is still in print and can be ordered from your local bookstore.

Pish, Posh, Said Hieronymous Bosch (pictured on page 122) by Nancy Willard with illustrations by Leo and Diane Dillon (and a frame sculpted by their artist son) is the ultimate children's book-as-an-art-form. It brings together an acclaimed poet/writer (her book *A Visit to William Blake's Inn* won the Newbery Medal) and two award-winning illustrators (the Dillons were twice awarded the Caldecott Medal for their incomparably lovely illustrations).

Hieronymous Bosch was a Flemish, fifteenth-century artist, wildly imaginative and known particularly for his bizarre, surreal visions of heaven and hell. Willard's story-poem is witty, delightful and matches Bosch in imaginative creation. The Dillons designed as well as illustrated the book; you can imagine the publishers saying, "It's all yours! Do what you want and make it a great work of art!" The text is hand-lettered, and shot as a halftone so as to preserve the shadings of tone in the calligraphic letters. The paper is especially fine and heavy, and the entire book very beautiful by any standards.

These three books, each so different from the others, are all nevertheless worth studying as art forms. If you are not an illustrator, you will probably have little say about how your text is illustrated, but keeping in mind how closely related text, design and illustration are in books for young people, an understanding of the whole book and a good background in visual literacy will enhance your chances of producing a publishable manuscript.

Here are some other books we think are worth careful study on your part:
  • *Zlateh the Goat* by Isaac Bashevis Singer and illustrated by Maurice Sendak is a book of short stories for children, an illustrated book, not a picture book. Although Singer said

illustrations might inhibit the reader from forming his own pictures in the imagination, that may be an old world view, not applicable to today's children. These ink drawings are Sendak at his best, and he captures the spirit of the East European Jewish culture that disappeared in the Holocaust. Examine this book for its unforgettable stories, powerful use of language and the best of the best illustrations that interpret but do not carry the plot. Notice the difference between these illustrations and Sendak's *Where the Wild Things Are*, which do carry plot.

- All of the books illustrated by the Dillons, particularly *The Sorcerer's Apprentice* by Nancy Willard.
- All of the books written by Nancy Willard. Different illustrators have illustrated her books of poetry and prose, all are well known and have different styles. Decide for yourself which combinations make the best whole books!
- *Alice in Wonderland* and *Through the Looking Glass* by Lewis Carroll. No matter how many wonderful artists illustrate this classic, and there have been many including Walt Disney, Tenniel's original illustrations are so much a part of the text that they remain the way we see Alice and her world.
- *Winnie-the-Pooh* by A.A. Milne with illustrations by E.H. Shepherd is another book with illustrations married to the text in spite of Disney's popular interpretations. A learning experience is to compare E.H. Shepherd's illustrations with Disney's animated characters and see how close they are and what the differences are. Then try to figure out why the changes were made.

You may prefer one artist to another, but never make the mistake of thinking one style is necessarily better than another. The beauty of contemporary illustration is in its diversity and the wonderful technology that allows printers to reproduce full color so accurately and provide children with a variety of good art. If you want to become visually literate, base your critical perception of the art on the plastic values: line, color, texture, pattern, form and composition. It is not enough to simply like an illustration or not like it. In order to be the best creator of children's books you can be, you should know why you like or dislike an illustration.

Notice the format, the quality of the paper, the binding, everything that is part of the book. It may be that the art is poorly reproduced or that the quality of the paper is so bad, it dulls the colors. Great illustration can be rendered boring and blurry by poor reproduction.

CASE HISTORY (BERTHE)

When I was teaching children's literature at Tulane, I used The Oxford Dictionary of Nursery Rhymes *and* The Classic Fairy Tales *and fell in love with folk tales and rhymes. Since then, I can trace every idea I've had for a picture book and even parts and themes in my young adult novels back to these books and the lesson plans that grew out of them. For example, the first assignment I gave was to twist a fairy tale from the classics and the second was to write down a rhyme the students had heard in the playyard and make a line drawing to go with it.*

I also used an old Celtic fairy tale as the basis for Lost Magic, *and I know I am not alone in finding inspiration in folk literature. All you have to do is look at a shelf of children's books and you will see that many of the authors have drawn from the classics.*

Here is a short list of representative eighteenth-, nineteenth-, and twentieth-century illustrators and their books. A study of the trend-setting books on this list can serve you as a mini survey of the history of children's-book illustration. You will encounter a wide selection of illustrative styles, get an idea of the times, and find clues as to what makes a children's classic.

EIGHTEENTH CENTURY: CHAPBOOKS, HORNBOOKS AND BATTLEDORES:

The earliest books exclusively for children were really textbooks to teach them numbers, the alphabet and moral lessons. Chapbooks – inexpensive, crudely printed books – were for adults but many of them were appropriated by children starved for story. They were illustrated, if at all, by woodcuts. You will see fine examples of early illustration in Peter and Iona Opie's *The Oxford Dictionary of Nursery Rhymes*. *The Classic Fairy Tales* by the same authors includes excellent

examples of eighteenth- and nineteenth-century illustration. If you intend to add to your library, these two books are great choices for understanding the roots of children's literature.

NINETEENTH-CENTURY ILLUSTRATORS:

George Cruiskhank, *Grimm's Popular Stories* and *Oliver Twist*
Edward Lear, *Book of Nonsense*
Kate Greenaway, *Under the Window*
Walter Crane, *Sing a Song of Sixpence*
Randolph Caldecott, *The House That Jack Built*
John Tenniel, *Alice's Adventures in Wonderland*
Howard Pyle, *The Merry Adventures of Robin Hood*

TWENTIETH-CENTURY ILLUSTRATORS, FIRST HALF:

Leslie Brooke, *Johnny Crow's Garden*
Beatrix Potter, *The Tale of Peter Rabbit*
N.C. Wyeth, *The Scottish Chiefs*
Jessie Willcox Smith, *A Child's Garden of Verses*

Kay Nielsen, *East of the Sun and West of the Moon*
Maxfield Parrish, *Arabian Nights*
Edmund Dulac, *Fairy Book*
Arthur Rackham, *Hawthorne's Wonder Book*
Kate Seredy, *The Good Master*
E.H. Shepherd, *The Wind in the Willows*
Wanda Gàg, *Millions of Cats*
Maud and Miska Petersham, *Heidi*

After World War II, modern printing techniques and the children's-book field exploded with a wealth of diverse, marvelous illustrators too numerous to list. This short list of illustrators who paved the way to the present and what we call "The Real Golden Age of Illustration" (the turn of the century is spoken of as "The Golden Age of Illustration" because it featured Pyle, Wyeth and Rackham) will give you a brief survey. If you are interested in studying more about the history of children's illustration, there are many reference books in your library.

When you come to contemporary styles, don't confuse classic with trend. What's popular today is likely to be passé or dated tomorrow; it's what the best-sellers have in common that you can incorporate into your own work. We see bright, clear colors, concise text and simplicity in books for the youngest; a bit older, children are reading by themselves and delight in the world around them. They are little sponges for knowledge and in illustration they see detail and don't like confusion. Still older children want action, mystery, adventure and characters they can empathize with, role models, situations in the plot that mirror their own and help them to see solutions. They still like illustration in their books provided the illustrations don't make the books look juvenile. Still older children have more definite taste: they like realism, fantasy, science fiction, even historical fiction as long as it doesn't play down to them or bore them.

Caution: Avoid imitation! Your study of books as an art form is meant to bring out the best in you. You are looking for inspiration and the best way to express your own ideas most effectively. Don't imitate a style in hopes of pleasing a child or an editor; look for new approaches that bring out what is uniquely yours.

Studying books as an art form translates into understanding how you can make your own book irresistible to a publisher.

WRITING OR ILLUSTRATING EXERCISE

Find a picture book you think is flawed and decide how you would change it to make it closer to an art form.

CASE HISTORY: LISBETH ZWERGER

On a crisp, September morning in 1983, I took the subway to a suburb of Vienna to see Lisbeth Zwerger. It had taken all of my courage and rusty German to call from the hotel and ask for an interview. I expected to see a middle-aged, worldly woman used to fame and fortune. After all, Zwerger had received a gold medal at the Biennial International of Illustration in Bratislava, two graphic prizes at the Bologna Children's Book Fair, and a New York Times citation for one of their "Ten Best Illustrated Books of 1982." When I got out of the subway in a nonplush neighborhood of shops and large apartment buildings, I wondered if I'd gotten the wrong address. But there was no. 7 and "Zwerger" was written under one of the twenty doorbells. I climbed the steps and on the fifth floor, the door opened. Surely, this was Liz Zwerger's teenage daughter who showed me into a bright, contemporary living room with a large sofa, a wall of books and an uncluttered artist's desk near the window.

But the young lady who looked like Audrey Hepburn in Roman Holiday was Liz Zwerger herself and it didn't take me long to realize that she was timid and as nervous as I was. I began by asking her how she became an illustrator. She told me she had been such a poor student that the only thing she could do was go to art school. But that answer like everything else about her was far too modest, and it came out later in our conversation that she had shown unusual talent as a child and that her father was a graphic artist. She had always loved Grimm, Andersen and Hoffmann and her favorite illustrator was Arthur Rackham. At art school, her teacher urged her to go into fine art, but she was only interested in illustration. I asked her if she wouldn't like to write her own stories as many illustrators in the United States do, but she said she preferred thinking about stories already written and channeling all of her creativity into art. Zwerger's paintings are the same size as the reproduced illustrations, and she does them in watercolor on watercolor paper. Her composition is striking. She uses lots of space around her figures and unusual perspective. Her colors are earthy; even her blue has warmth. The backgrounds are wash, and the figures more opaque and drawn in a brown ink line. She uses the kind of drawing pen you dip into ink, the kind

of nib that separates slightly when pressure is applied and produces a line of varying thickness, the kind you see in Hogarth and Daumier's work. It requires confidence and absolute control, no timid strokes. I asked her if she used models because her figures show such a thorough knowledge of anatomy but she said only when she has to draw furniture or animals. Lisbeth Zwerger is an illustrator who keeps alive the tradition of creating books as an art form and gives you insight into the "anatomy of success."

When you "take" step 10 in our book, you will read other success stories that echo Zwerger's passion and focus and see a color reproduction of an illustration on page 124.

Hooking Your Reader

"You can't judge a book by its cover" is an old saying meaning, of course, that you have to open and read a book before you know if it's good.

In choosing books, however, we often do judge a book by its cover, possibly consulting the book flap but certainly influenced initially by the title and the illustration on the front. School children almost always decide what book they'll take home from the library by its cover.

Think of a book's cover as a "hook," the term used to describe a device that attracts and holds a reader's attention. Many kinds of hooks keep the reader turning pages, and now that you've come this far, it's time to take another step and make sure your book is one that a reader will pick up and be unable to put down.

In the competition for the attention of a young reader, we have to be creative in our presentation of books. We're competing with the latest fads in toys, sports, movies and videos, to say nothing of the other books on the library shelf and in the bookstore! This is a tall order but it can be done using your ingenuity, by staying aware of what's new as well as what worked in the past, and by listening to what the child within, your most creative force, is telling you.

Here are the hooks that will attract the reader immediately: 1) cover, title and subject matter, 2) format, 3) illustrations. After you've got the reader's initial attention, the next hooks needed to hold that attention are within the text of your book. They depend on how you handle characterization, plot and tension.

Then, there is an invisible, intangible hook difficult to define that is the soul of your work. It is your point of view and passion that makes your book

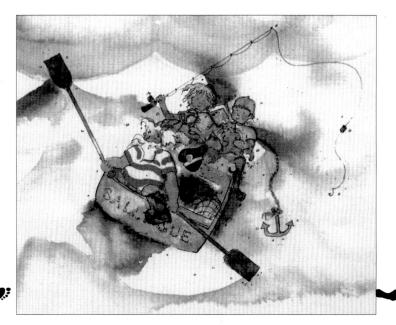

WRITING EXERCISE

In our book, Writing and Illustrating Children's Books for Publication, *we tried very hard to put hooks in our cover so you would want to read it as soon as you saw it. We wanted you to know exactly what the book was about before you even opened it, but we didn't want to use so many words on the front that the cover ceased to be graphically pleasing. What you see is the input of many people including literary editors and marketing people who worked with us on the words, and a graphic designer who gave us four different designs to choose from. Critique this book's cover and decide if it hooked you and why.*

WRITING AND ILLUSTRATING CHILDREN'S BOOKS *for* PUBLICATION

Two Perspectives

by Berthe Amoss *and* Eric Suben

uniquely yours. As you step along the way to perfecting your book, never lose sight of the vision you have of it, the most important hook of all.

Let's examine those very first hooks – the cover, title and subject matter. A cover or book jacket must scream, "Open me!" to a child, a parent, a teacher or a librarian. That means it should be striking and inviting in some way. The best way to make this hook your own is to study books in a bookstore. All of the jackets you see were first chosen by an experienced editor who hired a graphic designer or artist specializing in jackets. After that they were chosen by a very selective bookseller; everyone involved was thinking of how to appeal to a child or possibly how to appeal to an adult buying a book for a child.

Which covers do you gravitate to when you're choosing books? Why? Do you think a child would choose as you do? Think out the answers to these questions to understand how and why something appeals to you and why you think it might work with a child. Is it the color, the composition, the typesetting and layout, or all of the above that attracts you?

A knowledgeable graphic designer and/or illustrator has done the cover design, including the typesetting. Amazing things can be accomplished using different fonts, spacing, color, composition, etc. You'll notice that on a striking cover. These elements actually influence the "mood" of the book, which in turn is dictated by the subject matter and the intended audience.

It all may sound complicated, but the more books you examine the more expert you become in learning how to incorporate hooks into your book.

WRITING EXERCISE

Choose several books with covers that appeal to you. The books should be in the same category as the manuscript you are working on. Write down the hooks you perceive on the covers of the published books. Now plan a jacket for your own book. Even if you're not an illustrator, sketch a color layout, working in some of the appealing hooks of the books you chose.

Take every opportunity to examine many children's books to see what's been done and is being done. In addition to libraries and bookstores, there are several great collections of children's books open to people interested in studying children's literature. One of the best is the Lena de Grummond Collection of

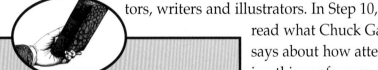

CASE HISTORY (BERTHE)

When I saw the jacket for my young adult novel, Secret Lives, *I fell in love with it. The original artwork was an elegant, large watercolor showing the interior of a Victorian living room with the three main characters in it. It seemed to me that the artist had interpreted everything I had tried to say in the text. It was a beautiful painting and looked mysterious, old-fashioned and intriguing. Two years later the paperback edition came out with a different cover showing an Afro-American girl and a white one rummaging through an old trunk in the attic. Again, another artist had caught the spirit of the book but this cover had a Nancy Drew look to it, promising mystery and excitement and was exactly right for the paperback market. Both very different jackets of the same book were great hooks, and the paperback went into three editions before it went out of print.*

Children's Literature at the University of Southern Mississippi in Hattiesburg.

Lena de Grummond, Superintendent of Louisiana School Libraries, retired at sixty-five and began teaching children's literature at USM. She realized that her students needed to see original manuscripts and illustrations in order to understand fully how and why children's books appeal. She wrote to the illustrators and writers she admired most, and undaunted by their fame, she asked them to send her an illustration of two or maybe an original manuscript. They did and the result is one of the most comprehensive collections in the United States.

In connection with the collection is USM's fine annual Children's Book Festival, which features top children's book editors, writers and illustrators. In Step 10, read what Chuck Galey says about how attending this conference helped him.

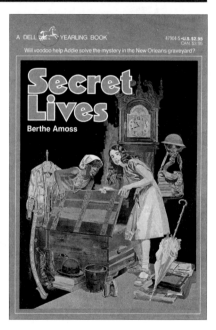

De Grummond's love of children's books and determination to accomplish what she dreamt of is an example of that intangible hook we talked about at the beginning of this chapter. Most people would have turned to grants to establish a collection of such scope, but de Grummond did it with a postage stamp and a vision.

Movies and books share common hooks,

CASE HISTORY (ERIC)

Your cover is all-important, but also pay careful attention to the layout and look of what's inside the book. In editing Eloise Wilkin's Book of Poems, *I placed the poem "London Schoolgirls" as the first selection. The picture showed uniformed schoolgirls in boater hats walking through a cobbled London street with a prewar schoolmistress. My boss liked the picture but didn't want it to be first – "It looks too foreign for our mass-market audience," she said, "and should come later, after they're already hooked."*

CASE HISTORY (BERTHE)

One of my most precious possessions is a copy of the illustrated letter Lena de Grummond received from Edward Ardizzone, my hero of illustration. He explained to her that he could not break up a set of his illustrations to send her one, but if ever she was in London, he invited her to stop by for a cup of tea. He didn't know Lena. She took him up on his invitation and returned to USM with a whole set of Ardizzone illustrations.

and as a writer you can learn from films how to keep our reader's attention. Good films don't let up – the tension may be created by characters or situation. Animated films are especially helpful to picture-book writers and illustrators. If you've seen a film recently that you loved, see it a second time looking for the hooks that caught you. You will begin to adapt them to your own work without even being conscious of it. Disney's full-length animated films are textbooks for you. *Beauty and the Beast* is especially fine. Buy it or rent it and study it for visual hooks as well as for tension, subject matter, characterization and dozens of other hooks.

Literary hooks come in many shapes. You need only visit a bookstore to see the growing trend to make books more toylike. Pop-ups and lift-the-flap books have been joined by books with toys, games, stuffed animals and cassettes attached, books that talk when you press a button and "feel" with textured material and "smell" with infused scent. How can a plain book compete with such an array of variety and delight? It must have a very appealing cover just to get the attention of a child and the contents must have enough "hooks" to keep the reader turning pages.

At Tulane, students of children's literature read brand-new books from the publishers to Newcomb nursery school children. The students then evaluated the books using quotes from the kids and sent their reviews to the publishers. "Read it again!" translated into a rave review, "I like your hairdo" was less than moderate praise, and a stroll away to play elsewhere was a bomb. "That picture is wishy-washy" meant that although it was a gorgeous

CASE HISTORY (ERIC)

When Berthe first broached the subject of a jigsaw puzzle book, I had no problem with the novelty as such. In the back of my mind, however, were my Golden Book thoughts: It'll be too expensive; we'll have to shrink-wrap to keep the puzzle pieces from falling out of the book. How can we design the cover to communicate the novelty at a glance?

The finished product, The Secret of Pirate's Manor, *was a delightful surprise. Clever production people worked it out so that the puzzle pieces fit tightly into the cover and cannot fall out. A gold seal announces the special feature right up front. Best of all, the book is comfortable in size, print and price, but wild and true in its demonstration that things fall apart but may come back together again.*

watercolor, it lacked clarity and had no appeal for a small child.

Pay attention to the age of your audience – the hook that appeals to an older child (a beautiful watercolor) may be over the head of a preschooler who wants to see recognizable objects.

You can get an honest evaluation of your own book from children but have someone else read it to them so that they won't be influenced by their feelings for you.

Don't forget that libraries can't buy interactive books. If your idea doesn't need an added gimmick to make it fly, your market is the library, where a book is still a book and the jacket, title and text are your hooks.

Above all, children do not like being bored. Work as many "hooks" as possible into your book without compromising your standards. As you write, you will become more involved in your story, and if you keep an open mind, more "hooks" will occur to you. When you "polish" your tension, possibly by withholding information, check your manuscript for each of the "hooks" we've talked about. Don't overdo it – just make sure your book will attract and hold a reader.

And so this fifth step on the road to acceptance is to make sure your manuscript has hooks, if not the cover then some device to catch the eye of an editor early on. Then, the text must hold the attention of a young reader, and so must have substance and hooks to keep the reader with you to the end. Make sure your book is your very best before you take the next step into the marketplace.

CASE HISTORY (BERTHE)

"I don't want her dumb old book!" the little boy screamed as his mother dragged him towards me. "I want this one!" In his hands he held an interactive picture book.

I was at a bookstore in Houston, signing copies of my then new book, Old Hannibal and the Hurricane. *Tomie de Paola had preceded me the week before and drawn all of the bookstore's customers. My following in Houston was thin to say the least, and the little boy was the sum of my humiliation.*

As swiftly as Paul's conversion on the road to Damascus, I made up my mind that my next book would be an interactive one that a child would beg for, and so I made the cover of The Cajun Gingerbread Boy *have a removable gingerbread boy riding on an alligator's nose. He runs through slit pages of Louisiana landscapes.* The Secret of Pirate's Manor, *which I did with Eric Suben, has jigsaw puzzle pieces on the cover. When the pieces are removed, they can be placed in the inside back cover to solve the mystery. I am still working on interactive "hooks" for the picture-book manuscripts I submit to publishers.*

CHECKLIST

If your manuscript seems dull to you, don't make excuses for yourself or it. Go through it with a red pencil and sharp scissors and erase or cut out boredom. Look for places where you might insert a hook and do it. If nothing occurs to you on the spot, tuck your concern away in a corner of your mind. After a couple of days, the answers will start pouring in!

CASE HISTORY (BERTHE)

This could be a difficult assignment, but invaluable to you. Persuade a teacher or librarian to let you make a presentation to her class of your book. Follow the format of my presentation using you own book.

A few years ago I was invited to talk to a school assembly of children from grades one through five. I was worried about what to say to six-year-olds that could possibly interest ten-year-olds. I decided to talk about book jackets and began by showing them the jacket for one of my own books, Lost Magic. *The story is set in medieval times, a fantasy about Elinor, the young daughter of Lord Robert of Bedevere, and her companion Ceridwen. Ceridwen's enemies accuse her of bringing the Black Plague to Bedevere and want to burn her for a witch. Diane Stanley's beautiful jacket shows Ceridwen and Elinor fleeing through the forest.*

Now, I said to the assembly, I am working on a sequel. It is about Elinor who is fourteen and an artist; she must marry a gross-looking man twice her age in order to protect her kingdom. It is also about John, a peasant boy of sixteen who yearns to be a knight but is trapped by the feudal system.

I gave the children a form to fill out and sketch in. Here is an example:

James C. Grade 4 #

CHOOSING A TITLE AND COVER ILLUSTRATION
for the sequel to Lost Magic

I.   Check the best title:
     (✓) Looking for Magic
     (✓) Searching for Magic
     (   ) Other:

II. Check the best cover illustration:
     (   ) John, the peasant boy, dressed as a squire with a
            knight on horseback, about to start the joust.
     (   ) Elinor, as a bride, getting married in the castle
            chapel.
     (   ) Elinor, in Ceridwen's tower room, painting an herb
            with a ghost-like Ceridwen looking on.
     (   ) Elinor and John together at the tournament, Elinor
            watching the joust, John assisting a knight on
            horseback.
     (✓) Other.

III. Sketch chosen illustration:

For the cover, Elinor as a bride was drawn by most of the girls and John as a knight was drawn by most of the boys (sorry if this seems sexist!). There were some interesting drawings of Ceridwen in her castle tower (one outstanding one is here reproduced), Elinor painting, John jousting.

What can be learned from these children's responses is that certain subjects are hooks: Children like magic, princesses, knights, jousting; they love action, a good story and mystery. It is a wonderful age to write and illustrate for, less crowded than the picture-book field, and more receptive than children twelve and up who would rather be caught dead than with "a book for young adults."

Reaching for Success

How many times have you heard this (ungrammatical) old saw: "It's not what you know, it's who you know"? Well, it's half-true – as true in the world of children's publishing as it is in any other field. One of the dark secrets of the publishing world is that sometimes people get published not because of their exceptional talent for writing but because they know key people in the business. You can make and develop contacts, too, even if you have never worked with or near publishing professionals.

First, a caveat: In any field of endeavor, what you know is of primary importance. If you know nothing, when opportunity knocks you will not be able to answer the door in a way that will assure success, or even a good try. Your skill and hard work are your best guarantors of success once opportunity knocks. But how do you get opportunity to knock? That's when who you know can really count.

When you want a job, you answer a want ad. When you want an apartment, you look in the classified section. When you need a plumber, you let your fingers do the walking through the yellow pages. But there is no such guide for knowing when a publisher needs a book. You have to take the initiative and make the publisher want you. A lot of the skills you need for this part of the endeavor are similar to those you need to find a job. You have to be persistent, polite, pleasant to talk to and meet, but you must stick to your agenda. Nothing must impede your reaching your goal, publication.

How do you find these great opportunities? Of course, you can start the traditional way, by writing query letters and sending manuscripts to editors whose names you glean from *Literary Market Place*, *Writer's Market*, or other source books. This process can be a long, slow grind, and it is difficult to differentiate yourself from others trying to break into the field. Wouldn't it be wonderful to start off with a contact of a more personal kind?

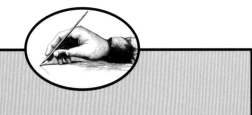

EXERCISE

Get started meeting children's-book people! Do one or all of the following:

- *Telephone your local high school, college or library, and ask about any extension classes offered pertaining to writing and/or children's literature.*
- *Read the book page of your local newspaper for news of book signings, author appearances or lectures in your area. Make sure you go and try to meet the visiting celebrity.*
- *Contact the Society of Children's Book Writers and Illustrators chapter in your town or the national headquarters, or visit its Web site, and find out about the Society's meetings, activities and publications. Sign up and participate!*
- *Contact the Authors Guild and inquire about writers' workshops that may be offered around the country.*

You can have that contact by working for it. Tell everyone you know that you are writing and seeking publication, ask for advice and guidance, and follow up every hint of an opportunity that comes your way. If you've ever conducted a job search, you know that after you've sent out a critical mass of résumés and been on a few interviews, the search takes on a life of its own. The cosmos seems to know you're looking, and you start to hear of opportunities in the most unexpected ways and places.

Something similar happens when you are seeking to get published. By putting yourself into situations where publishing and children's books are talked of, you will make surprising connections and discover synergies you never dreamed existed. That's why you have to do the hard work at home – write, polish, perfect – so that when you hear of people and places that may have interest in your work, you'll be all ready to go.

But they won't come looking for you unless you're very lucky. How do you find people in the publishing business? You have to network. Don't just sit at home. If there's a writer's conference, a children's-book speaker, a chapter of the Society of Children's Book Writers and Illustrators in your town, go to the meetings, introduce yourself to the people, and keep going until they know you, count on you and would miss you if you were absent

Let's start at the beginning. You are a writer without connections in the children's-book world. First you must have an idea of what you want to do with children's books. In Step 1 you answered questions about whether you are a writer or an illustrator, whether you want to write YA's or picture books. You should have refined your answers and reached some conclusions in the next four steps in this book. If you skipped these steps or still do not know the answers to these questions, go back and work through those earlier steps again.

There are several ways to get started. The first and most obvious way is to take a course in your chosen area of expertise. Contact a local school, college or library and see what writing courses are offered. Do any of these courses pertain to children's books? Are

CASE HISTORY (ERIC)

A well-run seminar at a first-rate institution can make a big difference in your career. During my first months as an editorial assistant for Golden Books, I wasn't sure the children's-book world was for me. I didn't know the literature, and anyway was far more interested in modernist masters like Woolf, Faulkner and Beckett. Then my boss suggested I attend a daylong seminar sponsored by the library school at Columbia University. To prepare, I had to read at least a dozen books on a reading list that was provided in advance. To find some of the books, I had to travel to the library of the Children's Book Council, where I soaked up some of the culture of juvenile literature. And some of the books made my heart sing! (I especially liked The Stupids Die *by Harry Allard and James Marshall, and Mercer and Marianna Mayer's* Beauty and the Beast.*) At the seminar, the keynote speaker was Maurice Sendak, who had just published* Outside Over There. *Although I had mixed feelings about Sendak's art, his exuberant, heartfelt performance on this occasion could leave no one uninspired. His devotion to his art and genuine interest in children encouraged me to go on and make a career – albeit a much humbler one – in children's books.*

there any classes in children's literature? Sign up and go. If you live in a locality without such a class, talk to the children's librarian or school librarian and see if she wants to start a discussion group or workshop. Even better, telephone the national headquarters of the Society of Children's Book Writers and Illustrators and find out if there is a chapter near you. Become a member – this organization sends out terrific mailings that help you feel connected to the greater world of writers and children's books. If not, find out how you can start a chapter.

If you are a librarian or teacher, you have a built-in base of information about activities related to books. Your teaching association or library association may sponsor events. The institution where you obtained your professional training may also run programs of interest. Read the professional and alumni publications that come your way.

Any class or group you join is only as good as the quality of your participation. Go into it with an idea of what you want. Always participate. Bring something fresh to share at each class, or make substantial changes between times based on the criticism offered by the teacher or your peers. Read in preparation for sessions. Even if there is no assigned reading, go to the library once a week and wander among the children's books, reading any that seem interesting to you. There are several different models for the best approach to interacting with mentors and other writers, and you should choose the mode that's best for you.

CLASS

In a class, you will be learning from an authoritative teacher figure. In selecting a course, check out the teacher's credentials. He or she should be someone who has been published and thus knows the terrain to be covered. Look up a few of the teacher's books before committing yourself to the course.

A writing class may combine passive learning with workshop participation. Try to absorb as much information as you can, particularly information of a technical nature, such as the layout of a picture book. The workshop portion may focus on only one or two students' work per class session. Don't be afraid to point out weaknesses in your fellow students' writing – that's how you all will grow. One positive attribute of a classroom setting is that the teacher remains in control and can make sure participants get equal time and no one comes away with hurt feelings.

WORKSHOP

A writing workshop is a more or less stable group of writers who gather routinely to share and critique one another's work. This setting may require a good deal of confidence on the part of participants, as there is often no moderating hand to make sure the discussion remains temperate. However, it is the honesty and outspokenness of the dialogue that is one of the strengths of this approach.

In a workshop setting, be prepared for criticism and frank discussion of your work. Although the process can be painful, it will teach you to take criticism – sometimes conflicting criticism from different individuals – and absorb it so you can reject the criticism you disagree with and make changes based on the criticism that is consonant with your vision and thinking.

Recognize that a workshop, although informal, is a commitment. Always try to bring something to share. Always participate. And treat the group as if it were a class in your punctuality and dependability. Look for a group that

CASE HISTORY (ERIC)

Berthe and I met at a children's-book event, and this book is one of the results of that meeting. After I left my position as Editor-in-Chief at Golden Books and entered law school, I had no immediate plans to continue writing children's books or being involved in the business at all. (The first year of law school is a rather overwhelming experience!) I read in the newspaper that Berthe Amoss was going to speak at a meeting of the Society of Children's Book Writers. I let myself be talked into attending. I had never met Berthe but knew her by reputation and knew we had some acquaintances in common. Also, I thought she had an intriguing name! I thoroughly enjoyed her talk, we introduced ourselves to one another and the rest is history!

shares your level of seriousness and accomplishment so you can learn and grow together.

WRITERS' CONFERENCES

A writers' conference is an occasional gathering usually put on by a large organizing body such as a university or professional association. The bigger conferences offer full menus of panel discussions and lectures on writing and publishing in all genres – from romance, to horror, to nonfiction, to children's books. When signing up for a conference, make sure there is a children's-book component, as all conferences do not necessarily include this topic.

You may incur a lot of expense traveling to and attending a major conference, so be careful about what you will be getting. Check out the quality of the speakers before you sign up. Are they people with good reputations? In addition to other authors, will there be editors and agents at the conference, and will you have the opportunity to interact with these people? Can you submit a manuscript and get a professional reading and critique? These are all questions

you should ask yourself when studying the prospectus for a conference you may attend.

A writers' conference is a brief, intense experience. Most last no more than a few days. Plan in advance to maximize your benefit from each moment. Go with a plan of action – who are the individuals you want to meet, when will you be able to meet them? Bring multiple copies of your work, self-addressed stamped envelopes, business cards and other materials that may be helpful to you and the faculty members you target. There are smaller writing conferences, too, often one-day affairs focusing on one type of writing or book. By the way, authors and editors like attending writers' conferences because they provide opportunities to scout for new talent. It's one of the few chances you have to meet editors in an

CASE HISTORY (ERIC)

One of the thrills of my life came when I was a law student. A classmate and I were standing in line in a coffee house in New Orleans. Suddenly a young woman rushed up to me and exclaimed, "You're Eric Suben, aren't you?" "Why, yes," I said. My friend was floored. (Later he asked, "Are you famous?") This young woman had seen my picture in the paper when it ran along with an article Berthe and I had written. The young woman wanted to know about writing children's books, saw me and seized the opportunity to introduce herself and solicit some advice. I felt flattered and didn't mind the intrusion. Don't think you'll be bothering an expert if one crosses your path – go ahead and approach him or her.

atmosphere where they're away from their desks and telephones and are actually looking for fresh faces. Make the most of it!

There are plenty of other settings where you can learn to meet people from the publishing business. Some publishing trade shows move to different venues each year. The American Library Association and the International Reading Association are two organizations whose conventions appear in different cities each year, and each convention is replete with authors, editors and other publishing professionals. Find out when one of these conventions may be coming to a city near you and plan to spend a day. Although the pass may seem expensive, it may pay off in the form of contact with people in the business. Your state library association probably has annual or semiannual meetings, and you should check out these as well – publishers send marketing people and salespeople to smaller conventions throughout the country.

Over the years, we have taught many workshops and classes and have appeared at writers' conferences in university settings and elsewhere. Our students have always been highly motivated individuals with all kinds of skills, including some they did not even recognize themselves. Through being teachers, parents, lawyers or whatever, these people had developed lots of abilities they could channel into creative work as writers for children.

We always insist our students submit manuscripts before attending our workshops, because writing is the best way for them to focus on the challenge of writing children's books. Sometimes the students are shy about reading their work, but by the time the members of the group get to know one another, everyone is open and willing to share. By far the most interesting remarks come from the others in the group, the "peers," and not from the group leader or supposed "expert."

If you attend any kind of event where a manuscript critique is available, take advantage of this opportunity to have a professional reading. If you don't have a manuscript ready to show, polish up an old one you have sitting in the drawer or write a new one in time for the event. You must try to get the most out of each opportunity, and the professional reader may know of someone who would love your story or may offer just the key words of encouragement or advice to get you started on an upward path.

Another way to get involved is to look for children's-book-related events in your community. Are there book signings by

CASE HISTORY (ERIC)

Do listen to the things the speakers say if you have troubled to go to a writers' conference. Once, while speaking at a small conference in Pennsylvania, I stated that a story with anthropomorphic characters could be successful only if it featured one of ten or so popular cuddly animals. After the speeches, each editor was supposed to meet with individual writers to critique their work. One of the writers who sought me out had submitted a manuscript about a flea. I cannot think of a less appealing, less cuddly animal! I had difficulty shifting my focus to offer constructive remarks.

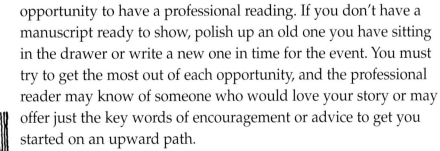

well-known visiting authors or local talent? Is there a talk at a school or library by a children's-book writer? Go to it, and don't be shy. After the talk or signing, talk to the celebrity. Without being pushy, tell him or her of your aspirations and how they started. Ask if you can write or telephone him or her in the future for further advice. Don't be afraid to make your goals known.

If workshops or classes are not for you, think about everyone you know and see if any one of them has a connection to someone in children's-book publishing. Chances are there is a friend of a friend who has some connection with the business. People are often happy to share information and contacts, and you should not be shy to telephone someone you don't know and say, "I'm Betsy's friend. I understand you write children's books. May I ask your advice?"

You may want to ask the person to read your manuscript or other material. The "expert" in this situation often wants to be nice and says he'll be happy to read your work. Go ahead and send it if you are invited to do so. But don't take anything for granted. As friendly as the "expert" may seem, he will be even friendlier if you allow him to respond in his own time, without persistent reminders from you, and if you supply a self-addressed, stamped envelope along with your manuscript so he can return it to you without trouble. Do not assume the "expert" has any interest in reading future drafts revised according to his comments. No more should you imagine – unless told otherwise – that the fact the person agreed to read one story means you have an open invitation to send any further stories. Be grateful for the advice, work with it if you can, say thank you and move on.

A modern way of making contact with the children's-book world is via the

CASE HISTORY (ERIC)

Writers try many different techniques to stay in touch. Staying in touch may be more challenging and important for people who live far from the center of publishing, so such individuals may need to be creative. One prolific writer moved to Maine but hit on the idea of publishing a monthly newsletter that would contain squibs about her upcoming books, samples of her writing in the form of short stories, and tidbits about the people she knew professionally. This is one approach to staying in touch with editors, though it lacks the personal touch. Also, putting out something as complex and regular as a monthly newsletter may become too engrossing an exercise in itself and take time away from serious writing.

Internet. The major Internet access providers have chat groups or bulletin boards where people with common interests can share ideas and insights. Look for children's books on your server and participate in the discussion you find. You may be surprised to find yourself meeting well-known figures in the field who are more than willing to share contacts and thoughts with you.

After you have made contacts through networking, maintain these contacts, but in a friendly and nonaggressive way. Send holiday cards and little gifts from time to time. Avoid telephoning, especially to individuals who work at home. As likely as not, your call will be interrupting work, leading to ruffled feathers. And don't expect people to be responsive each and every time you contact them. Keep up a friendly but remote contact, just enough to keep yourself in the other person's mind. If the person is an editor, when an assignment comes up, your card may be on his desk and remind him to call you.

One way to get an editor's attention is invoking the name of a common acquaintance. When making the first contact with an unknown editor, the writer may say, "Jane Smith told me to call you." Such an introduction can work two ways – if the editor likes Jane Smith, he may engage the writer in small talk about her to gauge the extent of acquaintanceship; and if he trusts Jane Smith's editorial opinion, he will likely invite the writer to send a manuscript. However, if Jane Smith is a competitor, the editor may be thinking, "If this story is so good, why isn't Jane Smith publishing it?"

Of course, you must actually have Jane Smith's leave to use her name. Such leave can be obtained at the time of your contact with Ms. Smith. When she says, "I can't use your story, but call my friend Ed Jones at Popular Press," you should ask, "May I use your name when I phone Mr. Jones?" If she says yes, go ahead. If she says, "Yes, but I don't think it will do you much good: Ed and I had a falling out some years ago," she is probably serious that her name will do you more harm than good in Ed's eyes. If she says no, the answer is no.

When you attend a workshop or seminar where you expect to meet people who may be able to help you, play to your own strengths. An outstanding commercial artist once came to one of our workshops. He brought along his portfolio and wowed the group, including us. We introduced this artist to some of our friends, and before very long he found himself dining with Maurice Sendak's agent! But it all started with his talent and excellent artwork. So what you know is still more important than who you know!

READING LIST

- The Complete Guide to Writers' Conferences and Workshops *by William Noble*
- Networking at Writer's Conferences *by Steven D. Spratt and Lee G. Spratt*
- The Writing Workshop *by Alan Ziegler*

GROUPS, ORGANIZATIONS AND HOW THEY CAN HELP WRITERS

Different groups help authors network with appropriate people and improve as writers. Barbara Shook Hazen, the successful author of literally dozens of children's books, has been involved with a number of prominent groups and organizations. Here are Barbara's tips about these associations and how they can help you.

First seek a writers' group or class. Barbara has been involved with the writers' group at the Bank Street School, which operates as a writers' workshop and sometimes as a collective – for instance, members of the group wrote many of the Bantam Easy-to-Read Books and the Golden Learn About Living Books. Clearly, membership in a group of talented professional writers can have advantages! However, this particular group includes only prominent professional writers; other groups exist that make room for individuals at an earlier stage in their professional development.

In a classroom environment, seek an excellent teacher for you – someone whose values, ideas and creative energy you like. You can also start your own group. Everyone in the group needn't be equally good, but everyone should be considerate. In dealing with classes and writers' groups, aspiring writers should work with people they trust but still take all suggestions with a grain of salt. It is important that the individual not feel "squashed" by the group. The other members should suggest but not insist. In order to give each member a voice, the group should not be too big – and it is too big when everybody doesn't get a chance to read new work at meetings.

The Society of Children's Book Writers and Illustrators is a good organization for beginners, providing information about how to get started and make contact with publishers, as well as a supportive environment for writers' groups and workshops. The Society also sponsors seminars and workshops with interesting speakers.

As you become established and better known, get involved with organizations that help authors with professional and business matters and provide information about contracts, rights and so on. Such organizations as the American Society of Journalists and Authors and the Authors Guild fit into this category.

Subscribing to professional publications like Publishers Weekly *can help a writer be conversant with what's going on in the business and begin to recognize the names of editors and other key players. However, such publications may offer a staggering variety of information to the novice just seeking to publish a book. In the vast, complicated world of modern publishing, the author must hone in on the information he or she needs.*

As time goes on, the writer may network less but become choosier in networking. That may be one of the benefits of success!

STEP 7

Plunging Into the Multilayered Marketplace

To market, to market! But which market? If you go to the cattle fair to buy a fat pig, you won't go home again, jiggety-jig. You need to situate yourself in the right market to write successfully. From the impatient writer's point of view, there may be something fortunate about the fact that the markets for children's books are quickly collapsing into one mega-market. Still, the differences in emphasis and style are worth knowing about if you are to sell your stories to the right people.

In Step 2, we tried to help you understand the different publishing categories that constitute the world of children's books. The publishing industry is also divided into different categories reflecting different segments of the audience for children's books. There are "educational" publishers, "trade" publishers, "mass market" publishers. Although the writer must be conscious of these categories or distinctions, there may be less to them than meets the eye. A person who reads all kinds of children's books must recognize that most are educational at some level. An affordable mass-market book teaches the satisfaction of owning a book, and this feeling is bolstered by the convention of providing a space where the child's name can be written following the words "This book belongs to…" In fact, any book that gives pleasure to a child teaches him that good things come between covers, the first lesson on the way to making a lifelong reader.

Think of all the levels on which children's books educate. Through maintaining high standards of grammar, punctuation, spelling, they communicate proper use of English. Through presenting the work of witty authors who use language with style, they communicate a love of language. By

CASE HISTORY (ERIC)

In my first months as an editorial assistant, I assisted a senior editor in designing a line of books for children one to three years old. I recall in particular working on a manuscript called "Baby Animals on the Farm." At the time, I was newly graduated from NYU with a degree in English, and my honors thesis had been about the novels of Samuel Beckett. The farm was pretty far from Beckett's wasteland! The manuscript ran that "cows go moo, ducks go quack," etc. "Little children really don't know anything, do they?" I asked my boss. "That's the point," she said, and taught me that books are opportunities for children to learn, and opportunities for writers to help children learn on every page.

retelling well-loved stories, they communicate the basic texts and values of our society and impart a love of literature. Through making sure that each page turn is motivated, that each thought is consecutive, they teach logic at a basic level. So children's books teach in ways beyond their actual subject matter, which might be about an educational topic (counting, alphabet) or just for fun.

Children's authors generally take every opportunity to point out something of value to know – the color of something in the story, for instance. Someone adapting Hans Christian Andersen might write the following sentence: "The ugly duckling had five brothers, each as yellow as corn." In doing so, the responsible writer creates the occasion for a picture that can provide the young child with an opportunity to reinforce color recognition and counting.

THE CHANGING "EDUCATIONAL" MARKET

There are school districts where funds for classroom resources have been severely cut back. The teachers in these districts have been known to fill their classroom library shelves with affordable Little Golden Books. The books are circulated, read aloud at story hour and ultimately distributed to the children at the end of the year.

Categorizing a book as "educational" does not mean only that the book teaches something. Rather, an educational book is one that is devised with teachers' curriculum goals in mind and that is promoted primarily for classroom use. It's a matter of marketing and not just of content. However, this market has been

CASE HISTORY (ERIC)

As I worked my way up the editorial ladder, I sometimes found myself editing books whose value was elusive. At such times, I tried to satisfy myself that the books had some redeeming value, that they at least taught something useful. One gross example was a story about a cartoon character named Inspector Gadget. I remember adding some action to the author's manuscript so that Inspector Gadget could wind up in a position to say, "Never play with matches." At least my conscience was satisfied that the story communicated something useful!

drying up as a distinctive segment in recent years.

The evaporation of a distinctive educational market for children's books has roots in the development of the "whole language" approach to teaching. This school of thought derives from the idea that children will be more interested in learning if they can glean information from books designed to interest children rather than from books expressly designed to teach. The philosophy is that trade books are written to engage children's interest and thus may be preferable to dry primers designed with a pedagogic purpose. Teachers and school librarians have long used trade books as supplements in the classroom and library. However, in recent years, these books have taken center stage. Thus, more and more mass market and trade books are finding their way into classrooms and school libraries, and such books' importance has increased in these settings. Philosophically one may have qualms about this use of books and its potential to take the fun out of books intended primarily to entertain. Nevertheless, there is no denying the impact of "whole language" on the market for children's books.

CASE HISTORY (ERIC)

When I was a young editorial assistant, one of my jobs was filling out information sheets on each of our new mass-market books. The forms were later provided to the marketing and sales forces to aid in their efforts. Among the categories of information I had to provide were selling points, which included the educational matter in the story. For a book like My Little Golden Book About Cats, *this aspect should be obvious – the book taught children about cats. For a book like* I Can Fly, *the challenge may have been more difficult – but some thought soon demonstrated that the book taught children to use their imaginations and enjoy word play.*

MASS MARKET VERSUS TRADE

EXERCISE

List the "selling points" of your story. Emphasize the following:
- *educational content*
- *format*
- *author's credentials*
- *illustrations*
- *interactive or novelty features*
- *popularity of subject matter*

Now write a graceful, concise letter to a publisher, pushing your story and emphasizing each of these features.

What do the categories "trade" and "mass market" really mean? Traditionally, trade books were high-priced, high-quality books sold exclusively in bookstores and to schools and libraries. Mass market books were homelier, low-priced books found in grocery stores, drugstores, etc., and almost never in school and library collections. These categories mean less as time goes on, considering that many, if not most, books are now sold in "superstores," à la Barnes & Noble, Borders, and Books-a-Million.

From a technical viewpoint, it was long the case that mass market publishers and trade publishers had different sales policies. For instance, trade publishers allow booksellers to

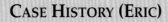

CASE HISTORY (ERIC)

A mass market orientation makes itself felt in every aspect of a book, including the design. Nonbook retailers often appreciate the publisher's efforts to present books in inviting displays that show off the wares while using a minimum of floor space in the store. Displays often contain pockets for the books, which means that the bottoms of the covers are cut off from view and should contain no important type or pictorial elements. When Berthe and I were working on The Secret of Pirate's Manor, *I thought the cover was great. However, it was designed so that the title ran in the bottom third of the cover. Though high-priced, this was essentially a mass market book, and I thought the cover design was a mistake. Every mass market editor to whom I showed the finished book agreed.*

return unsold copies of books and give a credit for books so returned. Mass market publishers did not take returns, which helped keep costs low. (It also meant that every book published had to be a "sure thing.") Now that the same publishing conglomerates publish both trade and mass market books, and the same superstores sell both types of books, such distinctions have become far less significant. Nevertheless, the categories remain as philosophical, aesthetic and economic constructs.

Mass market books are low-priced books published in cheap formats and distributed to both traditional and nontraditional retail outlets for books. A traditional outlet is a bookstore. A nontraditional outlet is a Winn Dixie, Walmart, or Rite Aid. In the nontraditional stores, books must compete with soap powder, juice and flip-flops. As a consequence, the books usually have brightly colored, inviting covers in popular art styles, with short titles that call out the most marketable feature of the book.

However, defining a book as mass market has more to do with philosophy than with format or price. An adaptation of Disney's *Pinocchio* is a mass market book even though it is presented in hardcover with a dust jacket and sells for $14.95. The book features a popular character in well-known situations and thus appeals to the broadest possible readership.

A study in contrasts may help illustrate the distinction between mass market and trade books. *Pat the*

Bunny is a mass market book par excellence. The cardboard cover is printed in baby pink and shows a squashy bunny. The title tells exactly what the child can do once he opens the book. The appealing word *bunny* is an important part of the title.

By contrast, Barbara Cooney's *Miss Rumphius* is a good example of the traditional trade book. The cover, beautifully painted, shows a lady in a green cape atop a windswept hill. The image is attractive but contains no element that is familiar, comfortable or irresistible. The title is cryptic. The reader has never heard of a Miss Rumphius, and is not given a clue as to why he should be interested in reading about her. The market for this book appears to be people who love beautifully illustrated books about adults, surely a narrower niche than babies who love bunnies. Because of its narrower appeal, *Miss Rumphius* is an ideal book for independent stores exclusively engaged in the book trade. Those booksellers are in the business of helping their customers find special individual books.

Traditionally, then, a trade book was a high-priced hardcover, with dust jacket, that had a somewhat esoteric appeal. Nowadays, with fewer independent book retailers, the notion of a "trade" book may be a thing of the past. It may help to call a trade book a bookstore book. Although the large chain bookstores stock mass market books, they also fill their shelves with more specialized fare. Those books that would look out of place being sold at full price in a Kmart are the "trade" books.

> *Only a few publishers put out mass market books as a matter of course. Knowing these publishers is important for you so you can research their formats and series and prepare your submissions to fit in with the editorial orientation. Here are a few:*
>
> | Publisher | Series |
> | --- | --- |
> | *Golden Books* | *Little Golden Books* |
> | | *Look-Look Books* |
> | | *Super Shape Books* |
> | *Random House* | *Pictureback Books* |
> | | *Chunky Board Books* |
> | *Grosset & Dunlap* | *All Aboard Books* |
> | | *Pudgy Pal Books* |
> | *Scholastic* | *Read With Me Paperbacks* |
> | *Simon & Schuster* | *Stickers 'n' Shapes Books* |
> | | *Chubby Board Books* |

THE SHRINKING WORLD OF CHILDREN'S PUBLISHING

The recent development of a unitary market for children's books has another source: mergers and acquisitions between and among publishing companies. Today the field is dominated by several enormous conglomerates that have resulted from large companies buying up several smaller ones or from one publishing giant merging with another. In recent years, Simon & Schuster took over Macmillan, which had a large number of children's imprints it had acquired over the years (for instance, Aladdin, Margaret K. McElderry, Atheneum, Four Winds). Penguin is taking over Putnam & Grosset (which includes Philomel, Platt & Munk and others). And so it goes. Although big companies like these try to let each imprint retain its distinc-

tive character, and although strong editors can help make that happen, there is naturally some overlap, some attrition and some duplication of effort. Net result: There are fewer places to submit your story.

Only a few publishers still publish only traditional "trade" books. You can give greater scope to your book's idiosyncrasies when submitting to these houses and others like them:

Orchard Books
Holiday House
Greenwillow Books
Philomel

It is also worth noting that some smaller independent publishers cannot afford to maintain their own sales forces, and their books are sold by bigger publishers' salespersons. This phenomenon also contributes to fewer meaningful distinctions among markets for children's books, although such small independent publishers may succeed better at keeping their special identities.

You must be aware of the different facets of the children's book market in order to understand where your opportunities are, but also to know where to submit your writing. A simple book with a universal, appealing theme should be submitted for mass market publication. A book with less broad-based appeal should go to a "trade" house. Although there may be some difference of opinion on this point, the same story can work for all markets if it is properly positioned for the target market. After all, mass market books have been written by Margaret Wise Brown, Ruth Krauss and other authors who are also well known for their acclaimed trade books. Part of the author's genius is in understanding which publisher can best serve which portion of the author's output.

You must decide how best to present your book for the market targeted by each publisher to which you submit your story. However, the steps you take to "position" your story may be less substantive than formal. That is, you may be able to make the same story work for publishers in different markets by playing up different aspects of the story's appeal in your presentation. For a trade publisher, you may want to develop a title and cover letter that emphasize the special feature of your story; for a mass market publisher, you want to underscore the universal aspects. For instance, a story called *Keisha Celebrates Kwanzaa* might work for Holiday House, but for Golden Books might be better titled *Keisha's Winter Holiday*.

For the writer, there are advantages and disadvantages to both trade and mass market publication. An expensive trade book may have limited appeal just by virtue of its price and fancy format. Adults might be likely to buy such a book for a special occasion or gift, or children might encounter such a book at school or the library. Such a book may feel less

CASE HISTORY (ERIC)

It is not always possible to change a story's title to position it better for a particular market. When I was editing Emily Arnold McCully's The Show Must Go On, *I struggled to come up with a more mass market title. The story was about a family of theatrical bears who retired from the stage to farm. The neighbors thought the bears were weird until they did what they were best at and put on a play in the barn. The universal aspects of the story were best summed up by the title* The Bears' New Home, *but this title cheated the story of its personality, theatrical ambiance and upbeat spirit. The fact that there was no mass market title for this book should have told me that it was not a mass market book.*

friendly and inviting than an everyday mass market book. On the other hand, a trade book's printing, paper and binding are generally of very high quality, and all the critical attention goes to such books. If prestige is your thing, a trade book should be your goal.

GUIDELINES FOR MASS MARKET TITLES

- *Do not use proper names of people or places*
- *Do not use foreign or strange-sounding words*
- *Do not use more than five or six words*
- *Do use names of cute animals where appropriate ("Bunny," "Mouse," "Kitten")*
- *Do use words or phrases that emphasize the universal aspect of the story ("First Day of School," "Grandpa," "Little Sister," "Jokes and Riddles")*
- *Do use rhyme, assonance, etc. ("Fox in Socks")*

Mass market books reach multitudes of children and are often cheap enough that parents feel no qualms in letting children have their way with the books – writing in them,

tearing them, chewing them. As a consequence of the need to keep prices low, publishers often settle for less quality in printing, paper and binding, and mass market books are almost never reviewed. However, these are the books that children handle and love, and often the books they remember best as adults. If your goal is communicating with children, mass market books may be the place for you. The economic consequences of putting yourself in one market or the other are discussed in Step 9.

A mass market publisher seeks to emphasize universality of experience rather than particularity of experience and to emphasize the broad appeal in the stories selected for publication. The function of an editor is largely a marketing function. The editor acquires books that will, he hopes, appeal to his audience. But he also tailors and designs the book in a way that will sell it to that audience. If you read the great mass market children's books, you will see they are every bit as strange as any other books but that the most universal feature is emphasized in the title and cover. Thus, a story about multiple generations in a Mexican-American family becomes *Baby Sister* for a mass market publisher. The same story might be *Aleta, Mi Hermana* for a publisher interested in calling out the special multicultural aspect of the story in order to appeal to teachers and librarians needing to enhance the diversity of their collections.

The writer is an important part of the marketing effort. You must understand the elements that make your story universal and the elements that make it particular, you must understand your story's educational content and its fun content, and you must be able to shift the emphasis in your presentation as you direct your story to publishers with different personalities. Markets are no longer as distinct as they once were, but publishers retain their philosophies, aesthetics and styles. You can play into these elements of publishers' characters by underlining different aspects of your work. It's up to you to show different publishers how and why your story works for them.

EXERCISE

Think of your favorite children's book. Think about the most universal aspect of the story. Now, in five minutes, come up with a new title for the story that will sell it to the broadest audience.

BOOK PACKAGERS

Books are marketed in other, more direct ways that reach schools and even into homes. Companies have book clubs that are advertised, with teachers' collusion, in classrooms. These clubs provide periodic circulars presenting an assortment of books. Some are award-winning trade books or classics that teachers feel comfortable will enhance classroom learning. Others are fun books that would appeal to children. Still others are published by the book club itself as "exclusives" and are available nowhere else.

These latter books are often prepared for the book club by a book packager. A packager produces books and sells them to publishers, who put their own imprints on the books and distribute them. The packager develops the book concept, contracts with the author and illustrator, does all the production work, and arranges for the manufacturing. Most often, the publisher buys actual copies of the book from the packager for distribution.

Generally a packaged book is most appealing to a publisher when the book involves complex creative or manufacturing challenges, unique editorial or art content, or when time is short. With shrinking editorial staff at many major publishing houses, packagers may become a primary market for aspiring creators of children's books. Your work must be "high concept," slick and thoroughly professional to appeal to this market.

If you feel confident about the professionalism of your writing, you can start selling your work to book packagers through submissions like those you would make to publishers or agents. Book packagers are listed in *Literary Market Place* and other industry directories. Some prominent packagers are Parachute Press, Mega-Books, Callaway, and Byron Preiss. Send packagers slick samples of your work and don't be afraid to follow up. However, be aware that most of the writing will come to you on an assignment basis, and the financial rewards may be different from those you could expect from direct publication. For instance, no-royalty arrangements are common with packagers.

CASE HISTORY (ERIC)

Usually it's the publisher that selects the author of a licensed character book. However, some licensors have lists of approved writers, and one must be selected from the list. One such licensor was Children's Television Workshop, producers of Sesame Street, *many of whose approved writers were writers for the show. However, at Golden Books we once received an unsolicited manuscript about Big Bird by an unknown writer. The appealing story won the approval of the CTW editors, and so* Big Bird Brings Spring to Sesame Street *came to be published.*

LICENSED CHARACTERS

Slick writing and professionalism also are needed to succeed in the market for authors of books about licensed characters or other "assignment" writing. Licensed characters are characters from outside sources like movies, toys or TV cartoons. Publishers contract with the outside sources for the rights to publish books about such

characters. Publishers then seek experienced, facile writers to write the books. Generally, there is no way to "audition" for such assignments; you must be known to the publisher, who seeks you out. But having submitted your own writing may be a way of demonstrating the needed virtues – tight plotting, knowledge of the picture book or other format – and may put you in a position to receive an assignment.

WRITING ON ASSIGNMENT

Other types of assignments might include writing texts for board books or cloth books for very young children; retelling classic stories; writing nonfiction books; writing easy-to-read or other graded books with very specific writers' guidelines. Assignment writing can be a lucrative approach to writing children's books, but the emphasis will be on fluent writing, thorough knowledge of formats and age groups, and deadline, deadline, deadline.

READING LIST

These well-known books were "packages" sold to publishers:

- Miss Spider's Tea Party *by David Kirk*
- The Wind in the Willows *illustrated by Michael Hague*
- Swan Lake *by Mark Helprin, illustrated by Chris Van Allsburg*
- The Story of the Easter Bunny *by Sheila Black, illustrated by Robyn Officer*
- The Cajun Gingerbread Boy *by Berthe Amoss*
- Jewels for Josephine *by Amye Rosenberg*
- *Sweet Valley High books*

When writing on assignment, use all your techniques to get started. Try to grab the reader's attention with your opening line, but also try to let that opening swiftly introduce the situation presented by the story and, if possible, the principal character. In retelling the story of *The Nutcracker*, a good opening line might be "Christmas Eve!" In some ways, it might be even more effective to write "'I love Christmas Eve,' Clara said with a sigh." Once you have an opening, write the story out and break it up into the pages of a picture book based on the page count provided by the publisher. Finally, write out descriptions of all the pictures and edit the text to complement the pictures you envision.

No matter what, the most important thing you can bring to market is a

CASE HISTORY (ERIC)

Golden Books had full-service editorial, art and production departments. As a result, the company was generally uninterested in exploring projects with packagers. I had started my publishing career as an intern with Ariel Books, a high-profile, high-quality children's-book packager. The Ariel people and I talked endlessly about trying to do a project together, but I was unable to overcome the hurdle of Golden's antipathy toward packaged books. Then, one year, our big Easter title was delayed by the illustrator's sudden illness, and we had a gap in our list. Right at that moment, I had a proposal from Ariel to do The Story of the Easter Bunny. *I called and said we could do the book if Ariel would promise to deliver it on what was now a very tight schedule. They agreed, and the book went on to be a best-seller.*

CASE HISTORY (ERIC)

In doing assignment writing, the author must be willing to follow the publisher's dictates. I once devised a series called Disney Classic Values, where each book recounted a sequence from a classic animated film and really pounded home the moral (for instance, Pinocchio learned the value of honesty after his nose grew). One author capably retold the story but didn't punch up the moral. I asked her to revise. "I feel like you're asking me to make the story didactic," she exclaimed, adopting the view, generally true, that didacticism is not a feature of good writing. "Exactly!" I replied. She put her personal preference on hold and prepared the manuscript to my specifictions.

good, well-written story. Editors fall in love with stories and will sometimes bend the rules of their particular markets in order to publish books they love. But be wary. If you don't think your book is a mass market book, try to avoid submitting to those editors. If you devised your book to be educational in the classroom sense, do submit it to the appropriate people. A book published for love often fails to land in the right niche. Despite the initial thrill of acceptance, bringing your goods to the wrong market may mean no one is happy in the end.

PERIODICALS

Periodicals constitute an entirely different market and so merit only a brief mention in a book about publishing children's books. Magazines are a good way to get your career started – to build contacts, gain confidence and land some sales. Another benefit is that publishers and agents will be more eager to read your first book if you have a track record of publication with magazines. If you have a story that seems right for a magazine, go for it!

There are several excellent magazines for children, like *Highlights* and *Cricket*. Writing for submission to these publications may be a good way to get used to writing for young people though less helpful for mastering children's-book formats. Thus, magazine writing may be a good short-term goal for the fluent writer of age-appropriate material who has not yet developed a visual sense or knowledge of formats. Most magazine stories for young people feature only one or two

spot illustrations, so your writing must do all the work of conveying the story. Like mass market books, magazines are meant to be consumed in the home, so your writing should reach children at their most receptive (although some of us will always associate *Highlights* with the smell of a dentist's waiting room!). Look for information on submitting to magazines in *Children's Writer's and Illustrator's Market*.

CASE HISTORY (ERIC)

You can put yourself in a good position to get assignments by submitting good original work to publishers. Pamela Broughton submitted a well-written religious story to Golden Books, and we rejected it as unsuited to our list. A year later, we needed a writer to retell familiar Bible stories for a new series. We called Ms. Broughton, who wrote twelve books for us.

Rethinking Your Story

If you have followed all of the steps we've recommended so far but you are stalemated by either a rejection slip or by feeling your story is not quite ready to submit to a publisher, you have several options.

You may want to resubmit to another publisher if you are satisfied your story is right. You may feel another publisher might accept your story as is. If this is the case, investigate further the types of books published by the new house you are considering. And be sure that after you've sent your manuscript off, you begin another story.

You can get to acceptance through persistence and luck. But persistence and luck are not things that happen to you by accident – they are the products of your own discipline and organization. Keep a log of all your submissions. Follow up with any contacts you make. If there is an interest expressed in your work, no matter how small, follow up on it! Send a note, or pick up the phone. Keep tabs on the peregrinations of contacts from publishing house to publishing house and make sure you maintain contact.

Editors come in all sizes and shapes and one may like the same thing another rejects. It takes two to make a book – you and your editor. It may take you a while to find the editor who likes your work but a good editor-writer relationship is essential to the success of your book.

If, however, you think your manuscript needs more work, try to diagnose its trouble. Here is a checklist to help you diagnose the problems in your manuscript:

CASE HISTORY (BERTHE)

I thought I had found a permanent home after I'd published four books (three picture books and one young adult) and had contracts for another young adult and a picture book, all with one of the most prestigious publishers in New York. Halfway through the illustrations for the new picture book and with the text written, copyedited and in galley form, my editor, who was also editor-in-chief and publisher, left and both my contracts were canceled. I was in limbo for six months while my ex-editor job-hunted. We had become close friends and I kept in touch with her. When she became editor-in-chief and publisher of another house, my two books were on her first list.

SUBJECT MATTER

Write about something you care about passionately, and know all there is to know about it. Make sure, too, that your subject is age appropriate to your intended audience. W.H. Auden once said that some subjects are only suitable for adults because they presuppose adult experience.

If you are unsure of what children of a certain age are like, get to know your audience. Richard Peck always talks with the high school students he is writing for, and he admits quite shamelessly that he has been known to eavesdrop on their conversations in places where they congregate. His dialogue is faultless; he knows how young people think and talk. Make sure there is no discrepancy between the age level of your intended audience and format or subject matter of your story. Know your categories! Refer to Step 2 in this book.

WRONG PUBLISHER

Make sure your type of book is the kind published by the house to which you are submitting. Check the *Children's Writer's and Illustrator's Market* and *Writer's Market*. Look at books in bookstores and libraries to see what types of books different publishers publish.

CASE HISTORY (BERTHE)

My first young adult novel, The Chalk Cross, *is a time-warp story set in my hometown New Orleans in the 1830s and in the present. It was written well before the Internet surfaced; I researched the 1830s in the Tulane library. I came across several books, fascinating firsthand accounts of life in New Orleans, written by Europeans exploring the New World, and there were two newspapers of the time on microfilm. I became so immersed in my young adult's time and place that I remember feeling disoriented when I walked out of the library. But when I wrote about the 1830s, I felt comfortable and confident I had my facts of time and place correct.*

Lost Magic, *a fantasy about an herb woman in the fourteenth century, required a different kind of research. I read everything I could about England at that time: Chaucer was wonderful and so were some firsthand accounts and history books. I also read and collected books on herbs and visited herb gardens in this country and in England, while growing my own herb garden. Research for this book was so engrossing that I caught myself avoiding the writing for the research!*

RESEARCH

Make sure you have done your homework and know everything you can possibly know about your subject! Research is fascinating – the more you know, the more you want to know. Use your library and consult your librarian. Use your newspaper, specialty periodi-

cals, the Internet; one thing will lead to another and there is no excuse for not knowing everything there is to know about your subject.

Be sure you don't let research become a substitute for writing, but don't gloss over it either. Read Whitney Stewart's essay in Step 10 about how she researched for her biography of the Dalai Lama.

POOR WRITING

Diagnosing your own poor writing takes humility, detachment and knowledge on your part. You will seldom hear an editor say, "You need to work on your writing." Chances are you'll just get a standard rejection slip, you know: "Thank you for letting us see your manuscript. Unfortunately, it is not right for our line…" And maybe your idea would have appealed to an editor if the writing had been good.

So how can you get a true evaluation? Do not think that because you've read it to your child and he loves it that it is good. Your child would love the telephone book if you read it to her.

A true evaluation can be had within a good writer's group or in a creative writing class. Join one or take a course. Perhaps you know a friend who is a professional and will read your manuscript. Take a course, read as

CASE HISTORY (BERTHE)

In 1979, I accompanied my husband, a shipping executive, along with a maritime lawyer and his wife to China. We went as guests of the China National Shipping Company, COSCO. The Chinese didn't know what to do with the wives, so they gave us a car and a driver and turned us loose. One of the first places we went was to a bookstore in Beijing. I stood there and watched children run into the store, buy what looked like comic books and rush out again. I bought the same and later with the help of our translator, I deciphered the text in the "comic books." It was the straight Communist line, painfully didactic, full of good guys (the communists) and bad guys (Japanese and Western Imperialists) and lots of fighting and violence; there was no allowance made for the sensibilities of young children.

81.   Some other enemy sentries were just preparing to fire back when the "head boatman" heaved a grenade at them, blowing them to bits.

much as you can and write. Reading refines your taste in literature and over a period of time, allows you to look at your own writing with a detached, critical eye. You will become so skilled in self-editing that you never submit a poorly written manuscript.

Write! Keeping a journal or writing daily is just like practicing the piano – you improve! Notice in Step 10 how many of these successful people "apprenticed" in writing and illustrating before they tackled a book for children.

THEME

What are you trying to say? Is it worth saying? Is it dear to your heart? Is it so dear to your heart that you produced a little sermon? Children will not read something that doesn't appeal to them voluntarily. If they are forced to do so, they will not take it to heart. Let your "message" develop from the story you want to tell. Don't preach!

If you tell a good story, theme takes care of itself and emerges. Every writer has his own style. Some writers start with a story they want to tell. Yours may begin with an idea. Just be sure that if it does, you don't confuse theme with message!

Be sure you present ideas to children and show them how to assess values rather than dictate to them which beliefs and actions are politically correct. Good literature is never didactic. Every good book for children teaches in that it enriches a child's life, but beware the book with a strong, didactic message, and don't let your own prejudices become more important than the story you want to tell. Good books teach children how to think, not what to think.

CASE HISTORY (BERTHE)

Susan Larson, the Book Editor at The Times-Picayune, *would slash my monthly column unmercifully to meet space requirements. It seemed to me she always deleted the part I loved most, but I learned what the word "succinct" meant, how to eliminate unnecessary words and ideas so that what I really wanted to say fit my limited space. Journalism is a great school for writing. Mark Twain was a journalist!*

WORDS

Never, never use an unnecessary word; particularly avoid clichés and too many adjectives and adverbs. Try to fit the adverb into the verb (instead of "ran fast" use "dashed"). Eliminate entirely the words "pretty" and "beautiful." Instead, describe a beautiful object or character as you would for a blind person and let the reader think "pretty" and "beautiful."

PLOT

Make sure you hook your reader in the first paragraph. Try eliminating the beginning of your story and starting wherever your story gets interesting. Vital information in what you've eliminated can always be worked in later in the story. Some of that withheld information may even add to the tension or suspense and keep the reader turning pages to find out how or why. Basically a plot should move inexorably forward from the beginning

WRITING EXERCISE

Look at the book you are writing and see how many adjectives and adverbs you can incorporate into nouns and verbs. Lop off the first paragraph of your story and work in the necessary information you deleted later in the story.

through the middle to the end. Make sure after you've hooked your reader in the beginning that you don't lose her in the middle. How many books you've read begin in a promising way and bog down in the middle? Keep up that tension; keep your reader turning pages to find out what happens next, and be sure you know where you're going, that is, be sure your ending is satisfying, the natural outcome of events that lead up to it. (Here is where an outline you make in the beginning will help you!)

WRITING EXERCISE

Make an annotated table of contents chapter by chapter for your book, outlining everything in each chapter if you are writing a chapter book. Check to see if your story moves forward. Eliminate digressions.

CHARACTERIZATION

Two essential ideas to remember from the start: make your reader care about what happens to your characters, and make your characters believable. They must never do anything "out of character." This is true even if you are writing fantasy, or maybe especially true if you are writing fantasy, since your fantasy will have its own set of rules and the limitations of whatever fantastic world you have set up.

STYLE AND GRAMMAR

Mistakes in grammar, punctuation and spelling are unforgivable and enough to turn an editor away from an otherwise interesting manuscript. If you're weak here, have a competent person check your manuscript, and use the spelling check on your computer. In the meantime, procure a book such as *The Elements of Style* by Strunk and White and Ken McCrory's *Telling Writing* and study them. Refer to our book, *Writing and Illustrating Children's Books for Publication*. If you are to be a writer you must understand how to use language!

Writing is a paradox – it can be the greatest pleasure if you have something you're dying to communicate and know how to say it in written words. Or it can be pure frustration, a medieval torture if you are writing about some-

WRITING EXERCISE

If you are not sure your characters measure up, write a character sketch for yourself only, and get to know this person you've created. If you don't really know him as well as you know yourself, you can bet your reader won't care what happens to him.

thing you don't understand fully or care about sufficiently, or if you don't possess the writing skill to express yourself. But all of the above are "correctable" and the skills you need "teachable." You can learn writing skills if you have not already done so. There are courses in both expository and creative writing at universities and through correspondence courses and at writing conferences. There are many books such as the ones we've just mentioned that teach writing skills and techniques, and, of course, as we've said ad nauseum, you learn when you read, not just occasionally, but constantly, all kinds of books and you learn when you write.

Writing is hard work but there is nothing more rewarding than being able to express in writing an idea you are passionate about.

One of the writers we admire most is Nancy Willard. Nancy is a poet who, in her own words, "also writes for children." She wrote *A Visit to William Blake's Inn*, which was the first book of poetry ever to win the prestigious Newbery Medal.

In an interview she told how she came to write *A Visit to William Blake's Inn*. "It helps me to make a model of the thing I am writing about. I suppose the most outrageous example of this is in *A Visit to William Blake's Inn*. Three things came together. An editor asked me to do a collection of poems for children. She said I could do them on anything I wanted.

"I had been hearing a recording of someone reading Blake's poetry, and I had a lot of it in my head. At the same time I was building a house, a very small house – well, not so small, it's six feet tall and it's in the dining room. I like to make things with my hands and I thought I would make a house and all the characters in it and that would be William Blake's Inn! It started out with odds and ends of found materials: broken dishes, jewelry, corks, old ashtrays, just all kinds of odds and ends, things from my scrap basket. The character called the Marmalade Man, a guest of the Inn, started out as a bright orange Burger King eraser, a little man with a crown, I think. He has since gone through many transmutations. That was the Inn. So I was hearing Blake's poems. I soon began to add a tiger and a few other things, and numerous angels, and then the poems began to be about the things that I was making."

WRITING EXERCISE

Write a dialogue between two of your characters. Do not use any description nor any adjectives or adverbs. Everything must be within quotation marks so the reader will know who's talking without "he saids" or "she saids." Here is an example: a conversation between a young mother and her eleven-year-old daughter.

"You are not leaving the house wearing those faded, torn jeans! And just look at your hair! It looks like a bird nest."

" I wouldn't be caught dead in that ruffled Sunday school dress you put out for me, and it took me all morning to do my hair. You just don't have a clue about how you're supposed to look at a party!"

WRITING EXERCISE

Experiment by changing point of view in your own story or in one you have read.

If you are an illustrator, your pictorial voice is equally important. You are translating words and ideas into pictures and every picture should tell a story. Before the Disney artist produced the conceptual sketches for Beast in the film Beauty and the Beast, *he studied and sketched gorillas in the zoo. Then he watched the facial expressions of the actor who read the part of the Beast, and in his own drawings, he translated those human expressions into his drawings of the Beast. The result is a unique creature, a humanized beast whose "visual voice" is meant to be and is very appealing.*

We can learn from this wonderful glimpse of the creative process how we can approach our own work from the beginning or when we're rethinking a story.

VOICE AND POINT OF VIEW

Chuck Galey is one of our contributors in this book. He is a graphic illustrator who has participated in our workshops, first as a student and later as a presenter, and is now in the process of making a transition from advertising art to book illustration.

Chuck was preparing for a second visit to New York publishers, and he was working on his portfolio and making appointments with editors and art directors. He was also rereading our book *Writing and Illustrating Children's Books for Publication – Two Perspectives.* "It's a funny thing," he said, "but, knowing you both, as I read your book I can hear Berthe and Eric talking, and I can tell Berthe's voice from Eric's!"

This we thought was a terrific compliment because we are talking directly to our readers in our "two-perspectives" voices. Voice is an important aspect of writing in every genre and you should try to hear the voice or voices in your own work. In fiction, the reader should hear a character's voice, and it should tell the reader more about the character than a two-page description. Dialogue often carries part of the plot.

WRITING EXERCISE

Read the first two pages of Charlotte's Web, *close the book and rewrite the conversation between Fern and her father, coming as close as you can to E.B. White's words. Now compare the two versions of the same scene and you will see the strength in E.B. White's words and discover any weaknesses in your own.*

If you are not sure of the voice in your story, read Mark Twain's *Tom Sawyer*, or better yet, because it is a book valuable to you on many levels, read *The Adventures of Huckleberry Finn.*

Listen to Huck's voice in the opening paragraphs of Huck Finn:

"The Widow Douglas, she took me for her son, and allowed she would sivilize me; but it was rough living in the house all the time, considering how dismal and regular and decent the widow was in all her ways; and so when I couldn't stand it no longer, I lit

out. I got into my old rags and my sugar-hogshead again, and was free and satisfied."

Read the opening pages of E.B. White's *Charlotte's Web*. Study it to see how another master of voice does it. We recognize in Fern that lovable quality of sympathy for the underdog so typical of childhood and all too soon outgrown during adolescence in the name of growing up and becoming "a practical" adult.

Voice means getting into your character, feeling emotions and reacting to situations as your character would, and then almost taking dictation from that character as you write. Voice makes you aware of words and language.

Voice leads into point of view. Are you telling your story from the "omniscient author" point of view? First-person narrator or third person? E.B. White and Jane Austen use omniscient author and third person while Mark Twain uses first person to tell his story.

Look (or should we say "hear?") at the visual voices in Tenniel's illustrations of *Alice in Wonderland* by Lewis Carroll; each drawing of a character (Alice, the Duchess, the Rabbit) defines that character for readers forever. No other artist's interpretation, and there've been hundreds, has come close to replacing Tenniel's visual voice in Lewis Carroll's masterpiece.

Fern defends Willard the pig.

> Here is a list of some of the more important things to look for in the books you read and avoid in your own writing in order to rethink your story and produce clean, concise prose where every word counts, and your reader hears the passion in your or your character's voice.
> 1) Sentimentality
> 2) Too many adjectives or adverbs
> 3) Hackneyed words or expressions
> 4) Telling instead of showing

You may be tired of hearing us say "Read, read, read!" but if you want to improve your writing, critique everything you read. Critiquing other books and illustrations will give you insights into your own work and help you rethink your story.

Just because it's in print doesn't mean the book you read is well written. Play the part of editor or book critic: What would you have added or subtracted in the piece you are reading? Analyzing your reading as you go along may not be as much fun as reading with abandon (it isn't) but there's no better way to teach yourself discrimination in your own work and help you rethink your story.

ILLUSTRATING EXERCISE

If you're an illustrator, try your hand at caricature: Find a photo of a famous person and sketch a portrait, emphasizing the important features (a prominent chin, a characteristic expression). Now find a good photo of an animal and "humanize" it without losing its animal characteristics. You might try your hand at this even if you're not an illustrator.

Study good, concise prose works of any of the following authors: Jane Austen, Beatrix Potter, Wanda Gàg, E.B. White, Margaret Wise Brown.

Clean up your writing and make every word count. Never send out a half-baked idea. Satisfy yourself that after this step, when you send out your manuscript, it is your very best effort and you're ready for our next step, dealing with your publisher.

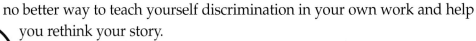

STEP 9

Dealing With Your Publisher

S tand up for your rights! These words should be the rallying cry for anyone contemplating an attack on the bastion of publishing. Business dealings with your publisher involve a matrix of your legal rights under the United States Constitution, the federal copyright statute, the terms of your specific publishing contract and common business practices in the publishing industry.

But you begin dealing with your publisher before you even have to start thinking about these matters. Before you get published, think about what being published means to you. Think about what you expect a publisher to do for you. Think about what you would most like a publisher to do for you. Is your top priority money? The look of your book? Just getting published? Have your priorities well in hand before you submit your manuscript and begin to make contact with publishers.

Have a vision of your book. When you see it in your mind's eye, what does it look like? Does it have full-color pictures throughout? Black-and-white line drawings? Does it have a special novelty feature that makes it truly different? If so, how do you communicate that feature so the prospective buyer will know it's there? Make a list of all the important aspects of the book, and keep it in your file so you'll remember your priorities when it comes time to communicate them to (and possibly compromise them with) your editor.

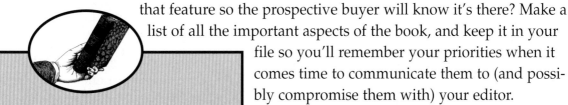

CASE HISTORY (ERIC)

Don't be afraid to be true to your vision of your book. Your priorities are important. Joan Elizabeth Goodman had placed her picture book Good Night, Pippin *with a well-reputed trade publisher. She came to find out that the publisher's budget was not generous enough to include full-color printing throughout. She pulled the book and resubmitted it elsewhere. Golden Books picked it up and published it to acclaim.*

SUBMITTING YOUR MANUSCRIPT

What do you submit to publishers? Of course, you should have your manuscript completed, thoroughly corrected for spelling and grammar and neatly typed in double-spaced lines on white paper. You should have an appropriate and appealing cover letter that introduces you in a couple of sentences and your story in a couple of sentences more. You should have a self-addressed, stamped envelope to enclose in the larger envelope addressed to the publisher. You may wish to enclose a book dummy showing your concept of the book's layout.

Where appropriate, you may wish to submit sample illustrations (color photocopies only at this juncture). However, this will seldom be appropriate. The most frequently asked question by the aspiring children's-book writer is whether he needs to have an illustrator before submitting his work. The answer is no unless the illustrator adds a lot of strength to the book proposal. Is he or she a trained, professional artist? If not, chances are you should submit the story alone. Book illustration is a demanding discipline requiring a high degree of technical skill. If you have asked a friend or relative to do some pictures and have any doubts at all about those pictures, seek a professional opinion before hitching your story's wagon to them. When in doubt, leave them out. Editors know many illustrators to call on if they like your manuscript.

You should submit the illustrations when you feel they are an integral part of the book. Such situations might arise when you are the illustrator, or when the illustrator is a well-known professional, or when you simply cannot imagine the book with different pictures. Otherwise you may do your book more harm than good.

Although you don't need an illustrator and in most cases are better off without one, you should have a vision of your book. Listen to an editor's suggestions with an open mind. But stick to your guns when you feel you must. The best rule for editors to learn – and not all of them are taught it! – is that if something isn't wrong, it doesn't need to be changed. For an author with a vision, this rule puts a high value on making sure everything in your book or story is right – spelling, grammar, punctuation, logical

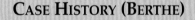

CASE HISTORY (BERTHE)

If you're sold on your idea, don't hesitate to be persistent. I knew from the start that I wanted my retelling of "The Gingerbread Boy" to have an interactive feature. I imagined the book with a small paper doll of the gingerbread boy, and slits in each page so the child could make the doll "run" through each scene. My editor wouldn't hear of it. But I persisted, supplying several dummies to show how the concept worked and case histories of how well the idea was received in schools I visited. At last the editor relented in "a Christmas gift": If I could make the story Cajun, I could have my slit pages. The Cajun Gingerbread Boy, *with my special feature, went on to be an award-winning success story, a Children's Choice selection for 1996. Some give-and-take may be necessary to get a project off the ground!*

sequence. By the time an editor sees your story, you should have considered each letter, each comma.

Writers frequently ask whether they need to copyright their stories before submission. The answer is no. Under the United States copyright law, a work is protected from unauthorized copying the moment it is written on the page. Publishers know this and don't court lawsuits. Anyway, it is unlikely your story is original, outstanding or distinctive enough for you to be able to prove a publisher copied it unless the publisher was foolish enough to copy every single word.

Aspiring writers are often concerned that if they submit their manuscripts, their ideas will be stolen. Registering your work with the Copyright Office will not prevent such stealing. Ideas are not protected by the copyright law, only the specific expression of ideas embodied in your exact manuscript.

Having your ideas stolen is one of the risks you assume in entering the publishing field; if you can't live with that risk, you should not enter the field. However, you should also be aware that such theft is rare.

The truth is that if your story is really very good and original, it might start a trend. Maurice Sendak's *Where the Wild Things Are* brought hordes of monsters and a certain look to children's books. There are still many illustrators whose styles owe a lot to Sendak.

Trendsetting is not

something you have to avoid. Just keep a step ahead of those who follow you!

There is another reason for waiting until publication to let your story be registered with the Copyright Office. Publishers have a commercial need to release new books every year. Novelty makes the books promotable and salable to booksellers. It may take a year, or even two, for a book to move from acceptance to publication. Add the time you spend placing the book with a publisher, and you may have a year or two more. Now your copyright is several years old before your book is even published, making it seem stale before its time.

Now that your submission is together, how should you approach publishers? There are two primary means of communication for this purpose, telephone and mail. (Avoid contacting editors by fax and e-mail until you are specifically invited to do so.) It can't hurt to phone ahead and try to

EXERCISE

Role-play an introductory telephone call with an editor. Ask a friend to play the editor. Your friend should think of the editor as busy, harried, about to go into a meeting and preparing for sales conference next week. Now what do you say?

Break your part of the conversation down into components:
1) *Introduce yourself: "Ms. Jones, my name is Fred Smith. I am a writer, and I have a picture book manuscript that might interest you."*
2) *Introduce your story: "It's a funny book about a group of insects living in a garden, but it also introduces a lot of neat facts about insect life."*
3) *Solicit a response: "Does that sound like something that would interest you?"*
4) *Say what you'll do next: "I will send you my story and look forward to your response."*
5) *Close politely: "Thank you for your time, Ms. Jones."*
What if the editor does not give the expected or desired response? How can you be polite but not take no for an answer? Practice a few methods and choose one that feels best for you.

arrange a meeting with an editor, or at least introduce your concept to an editor's attention. At this point, you're trying to generate some interest in your concept, so put your best foot forward. If you get an editor on the phone, do not address that individual by her first name until you are invited to do so. Introduce yourself as briefly as possible and try to describe your book in two sentences or less.

You have less time on the phone (or an editor's voice mail) than you have space in a query letter, so make the most of each second while sounding confident and calm.

A query letter is another effective way to introduce yourself and your work, but should be a second choice as it takes more time to write and more time to get a response. Also, many editors feel that since manuscripts for children's book are mostly very short, it takes less time to read the actual manuscript than it would to read and respond to a query letter and then to the manuscript itself. Overall, the poorest strategy is sending a manu-

CASE HISTORY (ERIC)

Be conscious of all the choices you make as a writer and of the effects they produce on readers. Authors with distinctive writing styles may be misunderstood. Jan Wahl has an unusual, lyrical way of writing that sounds slightly foreign to the American ear. When he submitted Tim Kitten and the Red Cupboard *to Golden Books, the editor asked him to do several revisions. But what was really bothering her was Jan's writing. At last, Jan sensed this difficulty and responded with a multi-page manifesto explaining his style and the conscious choices he made in crafting his writing. Golden Books never published that story, but my enhanced understanding of and respect for Jan's artistry led to the publication of numerous books by him.*

script "cold," without a prior telephone call or letter. Your unsolicited manuscript will be placed in the "slush" pile and become the lowest item on the publisher's list of priorities.

Your business dealings with your publisher begin in earnest after you submit your manuscript, and your dealings must be just that – business. Although writing is an intensely personal venture, once you start to seek publication, you are entering the publishing world as a business person and must be professional and realistic in your expectations and dealings. After you send your manuscript, your first communication may be a bare acknowledgment that your material has been received. Later, you may

receive a request to revise "on spec," which means you will not be compensated or placed under contract until and unless the revision meets with the editor's approval. You may be asked to make speculative revisions several times, so be aware

when you feel it is time to draw the line and either "fish or cut bait" (i.e., get an offer of a contract or withdraw your story).

You may or may not be a good judge of your ability to handle the formal, financial and contractual aspects of a publishing relationship. (Some of the skills are similar to those needed to have a successful marriage.) If you have any doubts at all about your ability to

EXERCISE

Imagine you are an editor and criticize your own manuscript. Write down the criticisms. (If you are not sufficiently objective or self-critical, ask a friend or several friends to critique your story.) Think about:

- *plot*
- *vocabulary*
- *length*
- *format*
- *theme*
- *style*
- *logic*
- *spelling*
- *grammar*
- *punctuation*

Now respond to each criticism. Write out your answers and make the appropriate changes in your story.

remain calm and cool under pressure, and to have your own best interest at heart even while negotiating a compromise, you may wish to consider obtaining an agent.

An agent first of all provides an objective eye on your manuscript or proposal and tells you how to retool your presentation to be most appealing. The agent knows the appropriate editors to send your work to, and has relationships with those editors. Once there is strong interest in your story, the agent's role may change. You may prefer to work directly with the editor (the editor will almost always prefer this arrangement), or you may prefer to work through the agent. The greatest benefit the agent confers is taking over the financial and contractual negotiations with the

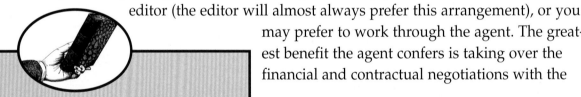

CASE HISTORY (ERIC)

Although publishers often prefer it when authors do not have agents, some publishers have been known to advise their authors on seeking representation. Jean Horton Berg had done several books with her publisher when she felt she might be better served with an agent to represent her. She asked her editor, Doris Duenewald (then of Grosset & Dunlap), for advice. Exasperated, Doris looked at Jean and said, "You're such a dope" (probably referring to the fact that Jean was doing just fine on her own and would now be handing over ten percent of her earnings to a middle-person), then got up and took Jean to the office of Dorothy Markinko, one of the most illustrious children's-book agents of her time. Jean was happy with the representation, and Doris knew that a favorite author was in the hands of a trustworthy agent who would not impede an existing relationship.

CASE HISTORY (ERIC)

One of my favorite authors, Jan Wahl, asked me for agent advice. Jan's brother had written a manuscript we had considered and liked at Golden Books but it just didn't fit with our list. After I returned it, Jan asked if I could recommend an agent for his brother. (Jan himself was unrepresented at this time, but had previously been represented by some of the best-known agents in publishing.) Mary Jack Wald had worked for some top agents and also been an editor and managing editor at Random House and Golden Books. At this time, she had just started her own agency, and I suggested her to Jan. She quickly placed Jan's brother's book, and Jan was so impressed that he signed with her as well.

editor, leaving you free to focus on the creative aspect of the work. The hope is that the animus that sometimes attends business negotiations will not color your dealings on the creative side.

You may feel it's tough to get an agent, possibly even tougher than getting published. The process of finding an agent is very similar to the process of submitting your work for publication – you must send out manuscripts, with polite cover letters and self-addressed stamped envelopes, and wait for responses. A big difference is that if a publisher writes back with a yes, a big part of your work is over. If an agent says yes, you still run the risk of the agent making multiple submissions without your story being

CASE HISTORY (BERTHE)

I started out on my own and sold my first book to Ursula Nordstrom of Harper & Row. I didn't know anything at all about publishing. All I knew was that I had been trying for four years to get a book accepted and that finally it had happened and I was deliriously happy. I also knew I was at a disadvantage because I lived in New Orleans instead of in New York. I could not have lunch with editors and chat with them; I was out of the circle of gossip and trends. I sold one more book to Ursula, and then I decided I needed an agent to keep in touch with the publishing world. I was able to get one of the best, Diarmid Russell of Russell & Volkening. But he knew nothing about children's books and so he gave me to his young assistant, Harriet Wasserman. Harriet became a good friend and placed many of my books; she knew all the editors and she knew what they wanted. But I never sold another book to Ursula, and I couldn't figure out why. Finally, a few years ago, with more experience and understanding of publishing (and Ursula), I figured it out. Ursula had been insulted. She thought I wasn't satisfied that Harper was giving me a fair shake and that that was why I thought I needed representation. Nothing could have been farther from the truth. So you must balance the pros and cons and decide for yourself whether you want an agent.

CASE HISTORY (ERIC)

When I was an editor, long before I became a lawyer, I would become alarmed if I picked up the phone and heard the words "I'm so-and-so's lawyer." Generally, I found lawyers did not know enough about the publishing business to negotiate realistically on behalf of their clients. And there was a time when a lawyer actually ruined a deal. A first-time Little Golden Book author somehow got a high-powered publishing lawyer to represent her in contractual negotiations. This lawyer asked me to send a sample of our standard contract, and I did so. She called up, made fun of our contract and characterized any author who would sign it as a "loser." Her client was the loser! I hung up on the lawyer, told the author I refused to deal with that individual and the book never came to be.

A PRIMER ON THE STANDARD PUBLISHING CONTRACT

Most publishing contracts contain standard terms that are conceptually easy to understand though written in tangled English. Here is a summary of the basic provisions:

1) *The author, the publisher and the work are identified; deadlines for your delivery of the work and its publication will also be included;*

2) *Warranty and Indemnity: You assure the publisher that the work is original with you; if this turns out not to be true, you agree to pay back any amount the publisher must pay the person whose copyright you infringed; you may also have to warrant that you will not attempt to have a "competing work" (e.g., a work on the same subject) published for a period of time after publication of the work under contract;*

3) *Copyright: The publisher agrees to register the work with the Copyright Office in your name;*

4) *Grant of Rights: You grant the publisher certain rights to the work under the copyright law – for instance, the right to print and distribute copies of the work, the right to make or authorize adaptations, the right to include the work in anthologies;*

5) *Royalty: The publisher agrees to pay you a specified royalty rate for use of each of the rights you grant it; the contract should also provide that you receive some advance to be held against future royalties, and that you have the right to audit the publisher's books as they pertain to your work;*

6) *Out-of-print: If the publisher ceases to publish the book, the contract can be terminated and all your rights returned to you (you may also be able to buy copies of the book or printing materials at a reduced price from the publisher's remaining stock).*

Publishing contracts typically run to five or ten pages or more, so there are many provisions beyond those listed above. However, this outline provides you with a basic primer on the nuts and bolts of what the contract tries to accomplish.

published.

In the past, many agents didn't want to represent children's-book authors. That situation has changed, as children's books have become one of the most reliable profit centers for many publishers. Editors may prefer to see manuscripts submitted by agents because such manuscripts have been prescreened, as it were, and may thus raise the expectation they are better than the common run of unrepresented stories. However, agents remain less common in the realm of children's

books, and you should not feel that being unrepresented puts you at a particular disadvantage.

Individuals with fewer problems placing their manuscripts for publication often prefer to retain lawyers to handle the contractual negotiations. A lawyer can be a valuable asset in this situation, but only one who is conversant with the publishing business and your goals. You will receive advice about your rights under the copyright law and about the effect of the provisions in your contract. A lawyer may tend to assume and present a worst-case scenario in advising you, so don't be overly alarmed by the possibilities he or she presents. You should also be aware that lawyers intimidate people just by virtue of being lawyers and sometimes by virtue of an adversarial approach

CASE HISTORY (ERIC)

It's important for your contract to be specific with regard to the rights to your work and how you are to be compensated for new uses. When Dorothy Kunhardt placed Pat the Bunny *with Golden Books back in the early 1940s, her contract was a simple two-page letter agreement. More than forty years later, Golden decided to package the perennial best-seller with a plush bunny to sell as a gift package. The contract made no provision for such use, so Golden planned to pay a royalty on the book only at the ordinary retail price and not on the much higher-priced total gift package. After a great deal of legal maneuvering, Golden was made to see reason and paid a royalty on the higher price – after all, the plush bunny was an "adaptation" of the author's work.*

al approach to even nonadversarial situations. Overall, a knowledgeable, credible agent is usually the best representative an author can have.

By the time you have a contract for a book, you probably have a personal relationship with an editor. You may feel the project will work only if this editor sees it through from start to finish, and you may be right. Books get published because editors believe in them and are advocates for them. However, editors frequently change jobs, and your contract is with the publishing company that employs the editor. Despite your preference, you cannot get a clause in your contract saying that if your editor leaves you have no further obligation to that publisher.

Nevertheless, contracts may be canceled by either or both of the parties. You may cancel the contract if you find you cannot finish or deliver the book, though you will probably have to repay the advance. Generally, there are penalties if the publisher has incurred any special expenses as a consequence of entering a contract with you. Pulling out of a contract for any but the very best reasons may have an adverse impact on your reputation (and could lead to litigation) and should be avoided. The publisher can cancel your contract more or less at will, though you will usually be allowed to keep your advance in those circumstances.

People often ask how much money a children's author or illustrator typically earns. First you should under-

CASE HISTORY (ERIC)

You always have some power over the fate of your work. We once signed up a number of books for an easy-to-read series on high-interest nonfiction topics. Later, the plans for the series were scrapped and we wrote to the authors telling them we were reverting the rights to their manuscripts and they could keep their advances. One author, Judith Herbst, telephoned me and told me she didn't want her rights back. She had written an excellent manuscript on the perennially popular topic of stars and planets. "I wrote this book to order for Golden, and I couldn't sell it elsewhere," she said. Her words got me thinking. I decided to hold on to the publishing rights and work with Judy to make her book a stand-alone title. It was published very successfully as The Golden Book of Stars and Planets *because the author wouldn't let us cancel her contract.*

stand something about how an author earns money. Before publishing a book, a publisher prepares a budget listing all the costs that will be incurred, from paper and printing to shipping and advertising. One of these costs is the author's (and, where applicable, artist's) royalty. A royalty is a percentage of the price the publisher receives for each copy of the book, and it is paid to the author after

copies are sold. The royalty may be figured based on the retail price, which is the price the customer pays to the bookstore; or the royalty may be figured based on the wholesale price, which is the price the bookseller pays to the publisher.

Before publication, the author typically receives an advance against royalty. This amount often represents the royalty the author would earn on the book's first printing, and it is paid before any books are sold. This money is to defray the author's expenses in completing the book and to demonstrate the publisher's good faith in entering the contract. After receiving an advance, the author receives no more money until the advance "earns out" – that is, until the publisher has experienced sales of the number of copies represented by the advance. In theory, if the publisher fails to sell enough copies to cover the advance, the author owes the publisher a refund. In practice, however, most publishing contracts designate the advance as "nonrefundable."

The royalty arrangement constitutes a type of joint venture between the author and publisher. Both assume some of the risk and some of the potential benefit of the book's publication. If the book fails to sell as expected, neither author nor publisher receives any further income from it. However, if the book reaches or exceeds expectations, the

CASE HISTORY (ERIC)

I have been involved in several projects that were canceled after they were a good way toward completion. Once we were working on a beautiful book by a young illustrator and were eager to sign up her next work. We did so, but it turned out that she delivered the first book late and that the artwork needed substantial reconstructive work before it could be photographed for color separations. Having lost confidence in the illustrator's ability to deliver the second book, we canceled her contract.

CASE HISTORY (ERIC)

I once commissioned a writer to write a new adaptation of Disney's Snow White and the Seven Dwarfs *as a Little Golden Book. Sometime later, Golden decided to blow up the book and republish it as a Big Golden Book. Under a royalty contract, an author might receive additional payments for such an adaptation. This writer had his lawyer contact me to see about a bonus for his client. But the copyright and the royalties belonged to Disney, and there was no obligation to pay the writer again. His fee was earned when he wrote the story.*

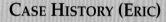

How Royalties Are Computed

Assume your book will have a retail price of $10.00 and your contract calls for a ten percent royalty. You will receive $1.00 for each book sold. If the publisher plans to run a first printing of 10,000 copies and pays you an advance based on sales of the first printing, your advance will be $10,000.00.

Now assume that the publisher sells only 5,000 copies. You have not "earned" half the advance. Good thing your contract says the advance is nonrefundable!

Instead, assume the publisher sells all 10,000 copies and prints and sells another 10,000, for a total of 20,000 copies. Now you have not only "earned" your advance, but you have earned another $10,000 as well!

author realizes an ongoing stream of income, as does the publisher.

Generally, if you are both author and illustrator, you can expect to receive an advance of between $3,500 and $7,500 against a royalty of one to seven percent for a small mass-market picture book. You can expect advances between $5,000 and $15,000 if you write and illustrate a trade book, with royalty rates between five and fifteen percent. Paradoxically, you can make more money over the long run with the mass-market book – publishers often print many more copies of the cheaper books and keep them in print longer. Divide all figures in half if you either write or illustrate. (But remember that in such cases the illustrator often gets something more than half – his or her work is considered, usually rightly, to be more time-consuming and technically difficult than the writer's, and to have a more immediate impact on a picture book's sales.) The less experienced you are, the more you can expect to start at the lower end of these ranges.

If you are offered a contract that calls for you to put up any money up front, think carefully before you write the check. This practice is known as "vanity publishing" and is not standard in the publishing industry. Although many a first-time author has been flattered when someone offered to "publish" his book, you should be thinking about the future and striving to make your writing so good that you will get paid for it. In a vanity arrangement, the "publisher" agrees to print your book for a fee. Such

Case History (Eric)

There are hybrid contractual arrangements. On Sesame Street books, where the author made a significant contribution, we sometimes paid a bonus after a certain number of copies were sold – a type of royalty. Dinah L. Moché, the astronomer, did extensive photographic research for the books she wrote, and she was paid a flat fee for that research although she received advance against royalty for the books themselves. But flat fee or royalty is the prevailing practice.

contracts may also provide that the press gives some promotional and distribution support. Nevertheless, your book will not get reviewed, will not get exposure in regular bookstores, and will not do you much honor. It's worth waiting for a regular publishing contract.

Sometimes a writer may receive a "flat fee," usually in cases involving assignment writing. In such instances, the author is paid for her work when it's done and need not wait for any books to be sold. Generally, the author in such cases retains no rights to the manuscript and has no right to participate in future earnings. Such an arrangement is sometimes called a "work for hire," although legally that may not be an accurate description.

There are ways to realize money from your ideas without actually doing any writing. There are several instances where well-known authors, editors or designers have conceptualized book series or formats and received royalties for all books published in those series or formats. For instance, Harry Abrams (who later founded his own highly respected art-book publishing house) devised the Illustrated Junior Library published by Grosset & Dunlap, and he received a royalty on every copy sold though the books were written by the likes of Mark Twain and Louisa May Alcott. From this it should be clear that publishing children's books offers a wealth of opportunity to earn money for the writer who keeps a cool head and stands up for his rights.

READING LIST

- Business and Legal Forms for Authors and Self-Publishers *by Tad Crawford*
- How to Be Your Own Literary Agent *by Richard Curtis*
- Kirsch's Handbook of Publishing Law *by Jonathan Kirsch*
- A Writer's Guide to Book Publishing *by Richard Balkin*
- The Writer's Legal Companion *by Brad Bunnin and Peter Beren*
- The Writer's Legal Guide *by Tad Crawford and Tony Lyons*

STEP 10

Success Stories

Throughout this book, we have presented case histories, true stories of how real-life authors and illustrators have faced problems and solved them. We believe seeing for yourself how others did what you want to do, is by far the best way to learn your craft. With this in mind, we asked well-known writers and illustrators to write short essays about how they first came to be published. We are thrilled with the response and think you will be too.

As we write, the market for children's books by new authors and illustrators is tight, and it is probably more difficult to get your book published than it was when these authors and illustrators started, but it will always be true that a good editor will recognize a good manuscript and good art if she or he sees it. Your job is to find that good editor and present him with your well-crafted book – a tall order but that's what our book is about. Remember, too, that these successful people were once where you are now.

As we put this book together, we grow ourselves, as authors, illustrator, and editor: our ability to discern "what works" in children's books is vastly increased, and it is this understanding that we are trying to pass on to you.

In this section, we will present examples of work by our essayists , case histories of illustrator's work, and examples of illustration that will help you discern that elusive "what" that "works."

We begin with the work of Katie Lee, a botanical and zoological illustrator whose extraordinary work and career began only eight years ago. Her seven books for children, all published in the last four years, include: *Orca Song* (Sound Prints, part of the Smithsonian Wild Heritage Collection), *Who Comes?* (Sierra Club Books for Children), and *A Visit to Galapagos* (Abrams) pictured on page 109. In progress are illustrations for a book of poems by Ogden Nash (Bullfinch Press) pictured on page 110.

Katie Lee

Katie Lee, born in Kenya and now an American citizen, was classically trained at the New York Botanical Gardens, where she now teaches. Katie has written and/or illustrated seven books since her first one was published in September 1994. They include A Visit to the Galapagos *and* Puffin's Homecoming, *which won the Parent's Choice Award. Her work is represented at the Hunt Institute in Pittsburgh and in the Shirley Sherwood Collection of Botanical Illustrations.*

I was married in Ireland, moved to America, had three children and divorced, all before I was 27. I did not graduate from school, any of the twelve that I attended; when I was in the second form, the headmistress told my parents that I was uneducable. Deep down all I wanted was to draw, but I had no training, and I had to earn a living for myself and three children.

I became the manager of a flower shop in a supermarket, and later with two friends, I began our own flower shop. I was searching for some good training for one of our flower designers when I saw the catalog for the New York Botanical Gardens. It began with the Botanical Illustration Program and even offered a certificate! I signed up for a class in pen and ink illustration. Two years later I graduated with a certificate, and I was teaching in the program.

When the next catalog came out, something else jumped off the page at me – a trip to the Galapagos. Far too expensive for me! I was broke, every credit card was canceled, but my children had all gone to college and I had to go on this trip. Just before the deadline for the final payment for the trip, my daughter borrowed money from her father, and I was on my way to the Galapagos Islands.

We were somewhere in Ecuador, traveling on an impossibly bumpy road in a bus; my travel mates were botanists, scientists. The woman sitting beside me patted my knee and asked, "And why are you here, dear?" My mouth opened and out came "I am writing a book on the flora and fauna of the Galapagos." To this day, I have no idea where those words came from. Writing? I had not graduated from grade school. Drawing? I had never drawn a "serious" animal and I had only been drawing flowers for a short time. How could this be? But I kept talking about my book to anyone who asked, so to protect myself against the worst embarrassment and failure of my life, I began drawing and painting.

The paintings were all sizes and shapes on every tone of paper. The writing was, I thought, very clever. I anthropomorphized all of the subjects. My thought was that this would be a book for young children. I did not know that it would be necessary to know the precise age or that there should be consistency to the illustrations. I was struggling with the text when a friend reminded me of a quote from Goethe, something to the order of "Seize the very minute. What you can do or dream, you can begin it. Boldness has genius, power, and magic in it."

I got the job done and it was time to begin selling this package. I went to see Harry N. Abrams and there I was told the work would never be taken seriously unless I changed my name. Katie Lee was just too cute. My maiden name was Kathleen Meyvis Arnold Pugh, and so I stuck with Katie Lee. I went to see Crown Publishing, who were much gentler and told me the work was "interesting" and gave me the name of an agent. It took the agent six months to agree to represent me and, in the meantime, I went to other publishers getting more and more discouraged. Finally my agent sent the Galapagos proposal to Abrams and they accepted it. Proof that agents work!

Now there was a rush to tighten up the text and complete more paintings, much smaller now. I paid for the photography, my agent was firm in her opinion that whatever Abrams wanted I should do. This was, after all, my first book and the publisher was Harry N. Abrams. The text went through many changes and almost the entire advance went to photographing the artwork, but this book got me credibility in the publishing community and most importantly I proved to myself that I could do it.

There is no turning back now. My brush has to earn my living. By the end of 1997 I will have illustrated six books and written one, *A Trip to the Galapagos*.

Whitney Stewart

Whitney Stewart writes biographies and magazine articles for children, and she has just completed her first novel for middle-school readers. She also uses biographical material for interactive Internet programs for students in grades three through eight. She lives with her husband and five-year-old son in New Orleans.

Her books include: To the Lion Throne: The Story of the Fourteenth Dalai Lama, *and* Aung San Suu Kyi: Fearless Voice of Burma, *her latest title (pictured on page 123).*

FINDING MY NICHE

Stuck behind an elderly woman in the checkout line of a grocery store in Concord, New Hampshire, anxious to buy my boarding school, late-night-study snacks, I spotted a sign that read WRITE CHILDREN'S BOOKS. I couldn't wait to grab it. I was so impatient I forgot my popcorn, bananas, chocolate-raisin gorp and butterscotch drops. I just wanted to know how to get my stories published. This was it. I met my destiny in a grocery store. I even forgave my bad manners as I bustled past the frail, old woman to snatch up the sign before anyone else stole my dream.

I was in eleventh grade, and I'd wanted to be a writer since fourth grade when my best friend, Suzy Tewksbury, and I stapled together our first book of poems on flimsy yellow paper. Hers were much better. They rhymed. And her handwriting looked like that of a writer, all swirly and pretty. Mine was scratchy and uneven. But I had passion and unbending will.

I submitted writing samples to the people who made that sign, and they accepted me. Not the writing really, but me. Their letter said I could take their course to become a children's book writer. I didn't realize I'd have to pay money for my dream, or find time after French papers and loathsome trigonometry to write stories, but I was thrilled and relieved that someone else understood I was a writer.

I didn't finish the course. My homework alone kept me up nights. I despaired. I studied writers; their lives enflamed me. I ate up six biographies of George Sand and perfected my French. I read Proust, Hemingway, Woolf and Plath, and imitated their sentences if not their lives. A French, a Spanish and an English teacher understood me; all three led me through literature, through biography. But, publishers rejected the stories I sent.

I went on to college, learned more languages, traveled the world and got more rejection letters, the impersonal kind. Finally, a college linguistics professor guided my independent thesis on children's books. She suggested I focus on children's biography, and I turned up my nose. Too dull, I said. She persisted. I gave in. I spent the next eighteen months bored by fictionalized biographies. This was the early eighties, and children's nonfiction was nothing like it is today.

Then I read Jean Fritz (pictured on page 124). Nonfiction was suddenly as alive as fiction. I couldn't get enough of her. When I'd gone through every Fritz book I could find, I wrote the author herself. And, to my excitement, she wrote me back. And what's more? She understood me, my view of nonfiction for kids. She even wrote that we were "on the same wave length as far as biographies for children are concerned." She, too, thought most children's biographies back then were "pretty dull." She said she wanted to explore human nature and so satisfy her own curiosity when she wrote biographies. Her letter struck me at a heart nerve. Fritz could never have known just how she worked on my inner puzzle.

I still didn't know yet I would write biographies. I continued to send out mediocre picture book manuscripts while doing anything I could to be near professionals in the children's book world. I took a part-time job as a children's librarian and read my way through the collection, took summer courses on children's literature at Simmons College where I met dozens of my favorite authors, subscribed to the newsletter of the Society of Children's Book Writers, and learned editing skills working on a college publication.

After college, I became a travel agent in New Orleans so I could travel cheaply, and I begged my way into the job as publication coordinator of a travel newsletter. Finally, I published short travel pieces, but this only fed my desire to publish a book. And it had to be for children. Nothing could sway me. As a travel agent, I'd come home exhausted and out of ideas, so I wrote very little after dinner. Then I signed up for an evening course with Berthe Amoss, and I came home with new ideas. I had renewed fervor. But alas, my day job zapped me of creativity, and my stories lacked authenticity.

I was laid off from the travel agent's job (a disguised blessing, I know now), so my mother and I were free to go to Asia. This trip was the final puzzle piece.

After biking in China and eating dust for weeks, we flew to Lhasa, Tibet. I stood motionless viewing the Potala Palace where the fourteenth Dalai Lama once lived. I imagined the little monk scurrying through a thousand rooms, his worried attendants in pursuit. As I toured his residential chambers, I wiped my hand along walls hoping to touch his fingerprints that somehow remained after the Red Army invasion of the Tibetan leader's winter home. I wanted to live in Lhasa, to know the people, to belong to that rugged landscape, even if it meant having more nightmares and delusions from lack of oxygen.

With great regret, my mother and I did leave Lhasa, but we traveled on to Nepal, to the Khumbu Valley below Everest. This place too stole my mind, heart and breath. How could I go home after the Potala and Everest? I saw myself donning maroon robes and meditating at an unknown monastery like a renegade character from *Lost Horizon*. Was I trying to escape the mania of Western life, reconnecting to a past lost except to my subtle consciousness, or experiencing the spasms of the writer's newest inspiration?

When I returned to the flat bayous and sticky air of New Orleans, I knew I needed to find my way back to the Himalayan range. As much as I delighted in Spanish moss and sweet olive, my present mind was caught on a rocky slope above the marketplace of Namche Bazaar, Nepal. I'd write about the Dalai Lama, I thought, and learn history as it happened in the highest lands of the world. Few American children would have ever heard of the Dalai Lama, and his story was a rich one I would love writing and children would love reading.

And that was that! Instead of writing a fictional picture book about Tibet, I chose to write biography. The Dalai Lama's tale was better than any I could come up with then. This idea was accepted by my first book publisher in the summer of 1987, eleven years after I submitted my first manuscript. I flew off to Dharamsala, India, moved in with a Tibetan refugee family, and interviewed the warm and wise Dalai Lama in his modest home in exile. This interview was the first of many, and it launched my career as a biographer for children. As Jean Fritz taught me in her books and her letter, biography can be the vehicle by which a writer explores human nature and history, and satisfies her curiosity.

Chuck Galey

Chuck Galey was born in Greenwood, Mississippi, in 1954. He says that, "after throwing paint around the Mississippi Delta for eighteen years, in 1972 I loaded my car and drove to Mississippi College in Clinton. There I studied physics hoping to become an oceanographer because I didn't think that one could make a living as an artist." Three years and a transfer to Mississippi State University later, he changed over into Commercial Art as a full-time major.

He graduated in 1978 with a degree in Commercial Art and after working for a few ad agencies as art director, he became a freelance illustrator in 1985. A demonstration of how he develops an illustration appears on page 112.

GETTING STARTED

A child doesn't decide to become an artist. The natural creativity of children is simply a part of life. In reaching out to children in stories and art, perhaps I'm celebrating the wonder of a line drawn on a page. Ragged at first, the line, with maturity, becomes joined with others to form a recognizable image. My early fascination was with these images on the paper that I could create. My first work of children's publishing was in the church bulletin, or rather, on the church bulletin. It was drawn during church. Having survived a lifetime of Baptist sermons, my guess is that many artists have begun their career this way.

So, after a college degree in commercial art and a few stints as an art director, I became a freelance illustrator. But an illustrator of what? To make ends meet, just about anything from women's shoes to jet engine fuel pumps.

My wife and I began to read to our son as soon as he was born, and the wonderful tales and illustrations made me yearn to create books of my own.

I had found the end result of my illustration quest. But there was more to it than that. The stories we read to our son reawakened a child in me. One that had been kept quiet for too long. I wanted to tell stories from that child's point of view.

So, I began collecting and reading everything I could find on how to write and illustrate children's books. The University of Southern Mississippi hosts the Children's Book Festival every year in March. I attended and met some of the best writers and illustrators in the country. Receiving all kinds of advice each time I went, I found others who held such events. I attended Berthe's and Eric's Two Perspectives seminars and found them to be a springboard with their generosity and inclusiveness. Joining the Society of Children's Book Writers and Illustrators and participating in America Online's Children's Writer's Chat Group introduced me to so many wonderful people. Through their encouragement, I braved the journey to New York to show my portfolio, manuscripts and dummies to the publishers art directors and editors. One trip later, I finally landed an agent and a book project with Blue Sky Press/Scholastic.

One of the most baffling things about the children's-book industry is the fact that many of the decisions are made on how well the editors have come to know you. In my idealized world of how things should be, an artist or writer is chosen strictly on talent. This is not entirely true. Since this is such a personal and competitive industry, the editor or art director needs to feel comfortable with you and what you are capable of doing. If you can find an editor who is still willing to nurture you, then you've truly found a gem!

The sum of all this is a factor that can only be described as persistence. If you have talent, your percentages are higher, but sooner or later you'll hit on a company or someone who will be able to help you out and teach you a few things that you can use down the road.

The underlying truth of writing and illustrating for the children's-book industry is to exercise your child inside you, not how you think today's children will respond. You are writing for yourself, not for the children. This creates a focus that cannot be deterred when disappointment and rejections come along the path. It is all a learning experience. Once you've determined this on a subconscious level, then the journey becomes the reward and not the destination.

Emily Arnold McCully

Emily Arnold McCully is the author/illustrator of Mirette on the High Wire, *which was awarded the Caldecott Medal in 1993. Her latest book is a sequel entitled* Starring Mirette and Bellini. *Samples of her illustrations appear on page 119.*

FIRST PUBLICATION

I was encouraged to read and to draw from life from the time I was three years old. Before long it was also made clear that I must be able to support myself when I grew up. Fine art, therefore, was never a possibility, while "commercial art" was. In any case, I had a strong predilection for narrative, so most of my drawings and paintings were illustrations. I loved drama, action and character.

I rejected art school because I had so many other interests. In college, at Brown, I studied art history, which stood me in good stead later, and also wrote and acted in plays. Now, when I create a picture book, it is like writing, casting and performing a little play or film.

After college I took a few menial jobs with small advertising agencies. I also enrolled at

Columbia for a master's degree in art history, and began taking my amateur portfolio to every company with an art director listed in the telephone book. But the response was not overwhelming. I persisted, pestering people on a regular basis, for years. My first break came when Russell Lynes, then editor of *Harper's Magazine,* asked me to do drawings for a high-brow/middle-brow article. By coincidence, the next assignment was for a cover for a Harper paperback book. But work came only fitfully until I was asked to make a series of posters for a radio station that advertised itself in subway cars. The theme was children playing. I was lucky beyond my wildest dreams, and Ellen Rudin, a new editor at Harper Children's Books, saw the poster in that week and got in touch with me. She asked me if I would be interested in illustrating a children's book.

The book was a challenge and it led to another and another and before long I was making the round of children's book art directors with my portfolio.

Picnic, a wordless book, met with success, and I began to write children's books with greater ease. Finally, I felt that my two impulses – writing and drawing – were happily united.

When I submitted my usual line-drawing sketches for *Mirette on the High Wire*, Nanette Stevenson, the art director, suggested I "drop my line." I panicked, but knew she was right. Since then, I have been teaching myself to paint and my work is generally far more ambitious (and frustrating) than before. I have been able to integrate my passion for history by fictionalizing real persons and events in picture books for older readers.

Three years ago I acted in an off-Broadway play and now *Mirette on the High Wire* has been turned into a musical. The various threads of my life seem more neatly woven than ever before.

Mike Artell

Mike Artell writes and illustrates children's books and teacher resource books. For two years, he also hosted his own Saturday morning cartooning show on WWL-TV (CBS) in New Orleans. Mike's books have been widely acclaimed by Publishers Weekly, American Bookseller, Working Mother *and other major publications. Mike has also been acknowledged for his "exemplary service in the promotion of literacy" by the North Shore (LA) chapter of the International Reading Association.*

Each year, Mike visits fifty to a hundred schools across the country, addresses six to ten major educational conferences and conducts several teacher workshops. In between, he writes and illustrates an average of four books.

Mike Artell's books include a "glows in the dark" 'Twas the Night Before Christmas *illustrated with collage pictures (Aladdin Books), and* Weather Ways, Questions, Facts and Riddles *(Good Year Books) and* Legs, a Who's Under the Flap Book *(Little Simon).* 'Twas the Night Before Christmas *and* Legs, a Who's Under the Flap Book, *are pictured on page 120.*

STARTING OUT

I started out as a class clown. Actually, I also ended up as a class clown. In between, I was a computer salesman who, on a whim, sent a batch of terribly drawn, incredibly corny cartoons to a computer trade journal. Fortunately, the editors of that publication were looking for ways to "soften" the bland-looking pages of technical text and decided cartoons were a good way to do it. They bought nine of the ten cartoons I sent them and I was on my way to a new career.

Encouraged by my early success with the trade journals, I branched out into more general magazines and eventually into greeting cards. I created cards for a number of companies, but I had particular success with a small greeting card company in the Dallas area who also had a children's-book publishing division. One day, the art director from the children's-book division saw some of the work I had done for the greeting card division of their company. She contacted me and asked if I'd like to illustrate a children's book. Naturally, I said "yes" and got my first assignment as a book illustrator.

After I illustrated the book, I mentioned to the art director that I had some children's- book ideas of my own. She referred me to the editorial people who agreed to look at my ideas. They liked what they saw and, after several meetings and phone calls, agreed to publish six picture books I had written and illustrated. Since then, I've written and illustrated more than two dozen children's books and teacher resource books.

If it sounds like the process was quick and easy, let me assure you it wasn't. Although I created my first magazine cartoons in 1977, it wasn't until 1987 that I felt I had enough momentum to quit my job and began writing and illustrating full time. Even then, it took four years for my first books to hit the market.

I don't think I would have gotten to this point without years of experience in sales and marketing. As a former businessman, I realized that publishing is a business and that publishers generally accept or reject your work based on whether or not they think they can make money selling it. I know that sounds cold, but if you think about it, it's the reason any business accepts or rejects a new product.

Does that discourage you? Don't let it. It doesn't mean your primary focus can't still be on creating wonderful books. It just means that you have to create wonderful books that will sell. Think of it this way… if your goal is to write books, then all you have to do is write. But if you want to write books that people will pay money for, you'll have to keep your reader and your publisher in mind. Both want to receive value for their investment. The reader wants entertainment, inspiration, humor or information. The publisher wants a reasonable profit. It's a business and you ignore that fact at your peril.

Sales and marketing experience can be very helpful, but I've found other factors be equally helpful to prospective authors. Here are a few:

Enthusiasm… When you write something great, even if it's just one great sentence, allow yourself to get excited. Give yourself credit.

Persistence… Never, never, never, never quit. Eventually you'll learn what you need to know.

Terror… Terror is a great motivator. I find nothing inspires me more than my house note, car note and my daughter's college tuition bills.

Faith… When no one else will answer your phone calls, there's always someone who will listen.

Michael Dorris

The late Michael Dorris was the author or co-author of fifteen books of both fiction and nonfiction. His three historical novels for young readers are Morning Girl *(1992),* Guests *(1994) and* Sees Behind Trees *(1996). His first young adult novel set in contemporary times,* The Window, *will be published in the fall of 1997, and is in the voice of a ten-year-old character, Rayona Taylor, who appears at older ages in two of his adult novels,* A Yellow Raft in Blue Water *(1987) and* Cloud Chamber *(1997). He was the father of three young daughters, who were his toughest and hence his most trusted critics.*

WRITING FOR CHILDREN

As with so many significant doors in the house of my life, I entered the room of writing for young readers… backwards. In the late spring of 1991 Louise Erdrich and I had just finished a long national tour to promote our adult novel, *The Crown of Columbus*. The fictional tale of two reluctant lovers, a New England poet and a Native American activist, who investigate the "true" story of the clash of Europeans and indigenous cultures in the fifteenth-century Bahamas (as well as, we hoped, a lot of other significant themes). *The Crown* was a demanding book to write, much less on which to collaborate – and personally I never hoped to hear or write another word about Master Christopher again.

Then one afternoon I got a phone call from an editor at a magazine published by Scholastic. Would I be willing, she wanted to know, to submit a five-page story, aimed at fifth-graders, about "The Discovery" from the point of view of an Indian person of that time.

"I don't know how to write for kids," I truthfully told her.

"Don't write for kids," she replied "Just write the best you can."

I agreed to try, and one early morning, while visiting friends near Lake Sunapee, New Hampshire, I sat down with a pencil and paper and began, in the voice of a twelve-year-old Taino girl, "The name my family calls me is Morning Girl because I wake up early, always with something on my mind." So much for wild flights of the imagination.

The five pages – outlining a rivalry between Morning Girl and her little brother Star Boy, a relationship that took place primarily in the week preceding Columbus's arrival on the scene – were finished before breakfast. I sent them off to the magazine, they were accepted with flattering enthusiasm, and published in the next issue – a sort of Quincentennary postscript.

Shortly thereafter I received another call, this one from Elizabeth Gordon, recently named publisher of Hyperion Books for Children.

"You know," she said, "I think somewhere between the first three pages of your story and the last two there might just be a novel. And if there is, I'd like to see it."

"But I don't know how to write for young readers," I repeated.

"Yes," Liz said, "you do." She sounded like a person who knew what she was talking about.

"If I try, will you tell me honestly when I mess up?" I asked.

"You'd better believe it."

So… I did, she did, I re-did, and the result was *Morning Girl*, my first novel for young adults.

And the fact of the matter has been clear to me ever since: a writer doesn't write for a particular audience, he or she writes in a quest for a true and compelling narrative voice. If that can be uncovered, the question of age, gender or ethnicity is completely and blessedly irrelevant.

Amye Rosenberg

Amye Rosenberg is the author and/or illustrator of seventy children's books published in the United States and seventeen foreign countries. These include diverse formats like pop-up, board books, anthologies and interactive sticker storybooks. Among her most popular titles are Melly's Menorah *(pictured on page 116),* Good Job, Jelly Bean, Biggest Most Beautiful Christmas Tree *and* Jewels For Josephine, *the first picture book to utilize plastic stick-on "jewels" to teach the number one hundred and the value of sharing – all in one book!*

STARTING WITH A POP-UP

There is a lot more to a successful career in children's books than being a dazzling author/artist, though frankly, it helps! My first publishing experience taught me that having a comprehensive understanding of different formats and a willingness to accommodate the publisher's needs is as important as being a great talent. You must be well rounded too, willing to meet all challenges and to go where no artist has gone before!

The yearning to do a full-color picture book drew me to places where one might find a variety of material in print. One day, a friend dragged me to a gift trade show where I didn't expect to find much. I was surprised and delighted to discover a local packager of pop-up and other novelty children's books. I quickly made an appointment to visit their offices with my portfolio.

Having noticed the absence of an alphabet pop-up among their vast display, I decided to whip up a rough dummy of one consisting of sketches and even included a clumsy paper mechanical.

Their creative director was impressed with my initiative, but explained that since much of their business was foreign, all of their books had to work in at least five languages with only the black type changing. That was especially problematic with an alphabet/word format where the words for certain objects don't always begin with the same letter in different languages.

I'd come this far and wasn't about to give up.

"What languages did you have in mind?" I asked.

Quicker than you could say "Pat the Bunny," I was in the local library, tearing through French, Spanish, German and Italian dictionaries. Suddenly I knew why I suffered through two miserable years of high school Latin.

Word roots in the Romance language group tended to be similar, especially when referring to animals. By using international techno-terms (like telephone and automobile) and cross-referencing words and images in addition to animal characters, *Pop-up Alphabet Soup* began to take shape.

Within a week I returned with a workable solution, and *Pop-up Alphabet Soup* was on its way to publication!

However, there were more challenges ahead. Because pop-up books are multidimensional, I could not create conventional illustrations. Each spread consisted of the first page plus all the parts that would be assembled into moving elements. It was like illustrating a jigsaw puzzle in pieces. I had to work closely with their ace team of paper engineers to ensure that everything fit together accurately and worked. Who would have thought that a book that provides the spontaneous joy of pulling tabs, lifting flaps, revealing snakes that wiggle and lions that pull peacocks out of magicians' hats, would require the precision of a Swiss watch!

N
Nightmare

The finished, printed book went to the Bologna International Children's Book Fair and was printed in four (of the five) languages. It was huge exposure for a first effort, but being a first effort, my inexperience was evident in the artwork.

I knew nothing about using my palette for reproduction (the color was too muddy or too bright) and I'd never illustrated animals before so the images were crude and inconsistent. Financially, I received little for all the effort, but it accomplished so much more.

Pop-up Alphabet Soup was a strong addition to my portfolio when I went to New York to see the "big" publishers. They were impressed with how the book evolved. It was clear I wasn't just another artist, but a problem solver who enjoyed challenge and had a thorough understanding of format, so important in children's publishing where such a huge variety exists. This undoubtedly gave me an edge in a highly competitive industry. In no time at all, I was designing, writing and illustrating dozens of books in dozens of different formats!

Joan Elizabeth Goodman

I was part of the baby boom of the fifties. The Cold War, rock and roll, the Beatles, drugs, hippies and Vietnam defined my coming of age in suburban Connecticut. I went to Pratt Institute in Brooklyn, New York, as an art major. My sophomore year was spent studying painting at L'Accademia de Belle Arte in Rome. Rome has remained with me as vital and mythic as my childhood. My first novel, Songs From Home, *was set there.*

I finished a BFA degree at Pratt, spent a happy year as a clerk in an art supply store before Hallmark Cards hired me to draw fuzzy bunnies. After a couple of years in the Midwest, I returned to New York intent on illustrating textbooks and picture books to feel, if not wildly successful, at least professional.

I gradually became an illustrator who writes, and my list of published picture books began to grow (Eric Suben was one of my first and favorite editors).

I married Keith Goldsmith who works in publishing (unfortunately his company only publishes dead authors!). We have two children, Juliet, eight, and Henry, two. My family has given me the challenge of trying to work around their needs. I've found it easier to pursue the writing. A paragraph can be interrupted by a baby's cry with not too much harm done, whereas an interrupted watercolor could be ruined. With or without children to distract me I might have pursued the writing more intently than the illustrating part of my career. Writing opened a door for me into a realm of magic and mystery. It is a place I go to as often as I can. The writing has freed my art, as well. When time is available, I get out my oil paints and have fun.

To date my published work includes ten picture books that I've illustrated, thirteen that I've written and illustrated, one picture book illustrated by someone else, and two novels (with incidental illustrations). This year I've had the pleasure of seeing the publication of a picture book, Bernard's Bath *(Boyds Mills Press), an historical novel,* The Winter Hare *(Houghton Mifflin), two stories in* Ladybug *magazine, and the acceptance of my second historical novel,* Hope's Crossing *(Houghton Mifflin).*

BEYOND BEAD-STRINGING

I had been illustrating children's books for a few years and wanted very much to write my own stories. I particularly admired the writing of Arnold

Lobel. He had given life to two wonderful green and brown creatures. I had two creatures of my own, intractable cats named Micio and Lily. I thought they could become my Frog and Toad.

Writing was a slow, painful process, a sort of stuttering on paper. I'd been working with picture books long enough to understand some of the basic requirements: the length of the manuscript, the relative amount of text per page, and the importance of character, plot and theme. I recognized the charm, wit and wisdom in Mr. Lobel's characters, and hoped to emulate him. The problem with my writing was my disregard of a few other critical ingredients in a children's book: the need for strong and vivid action, appealing characters and ultimately a story that would interest children. My kitty characters acted out a Noel Coward, feline pastiche, that had more to do with my adult relationships than anything else. What's worse – my story was in verse!

However, I was persistent. I kept plugging away at versions of the Micio and Lily story. I wrote and rewrote the same inaccessible and inappropriate story. I felt sure that I was in the process of creating a classic tale of friendship to rival Frog and Toad.

While agonizing over arch dialogue for Micio and Lily, I drew my cat characters over and over until their images grew stiff and formulaic. Then I spent many happy hours doodling in decorative backgrounds – checkerboard floors, flowered wallpapers, stripes, dots! This was not so much a creative endeavor as the kind of therapeutic bead-stringing prescribed for the deeply disturbed along with their doses of Thorazine.

Needless to say, none of the variations of the Micio and Lily story sold. I was working diligently, but not getting anywhere. Around this time a casual acquaintance suggested a class for writing children's books at The New School. I'll never know what possessed me to take this person's advice – taking advice is not my strong suit – but I went ahead and registered for Margaret Gabel's Workshop in Writing for Children.

That was over fifteen years ago, and I've never missed a semester since. Ms. Gabel's class helped me find a way out of my tangle of cute cleverness into the real world of children's literature. Not only have I had the astute guidance of a compassionate editor in Ms. Gabel, I've also had the brilliant examples of my classmates to follow. Some of children's books' best writers have participated in Ms. Gabel's workshop. At first hearing the work of Pam Conrad, Pat Kibbe, Jane Mali, Alison Herzig, Patricia Hermes, Patricia Reilly Giff, was terribly intimidating. I saw that my stories were a long way from where they ought to have been. However, Ms. Gabel's class was and is about encouragement and support. I listened to the critiques of my work and began to understand what was being said. Even more significantly, while trying to comment intelligently on my classmates' work, I gained the necessary perspective on my own writing. I found that the bead-stringing I'd been doing with the illustration was pervasive in the writing, as well. Shifting words around, fiddling with synonyms and rhyme schemes wasn't really writing, and it definitely wasn't good writing.

After a year or so of Ms. Gabel's workshop, I wrote a story that sold! It was called *Right's Animal Farm*. It was about nice but compulsively neat Farmer Right who tried to impose too much order on his farm causing the animals to rebel. The story had no relation to the Frog and Toad books, but the inspiration did come from my cat, Micio. He had a tendency to quack when demanding more and better food. I'd say to him, "'Quack, quack,' said the cat."

Hmm, I thought, "Quack, quack," said the cat, "Meow," said the cow. Silliness, the child's point of view, all the good writing skills I'd been learning in Ms. Gabel's class combined to produce a real book for children.

Sample illustrations from Joan Elizabeth Goodman's book, Good Night, Pippin *appear on page 118.*

Richard Egielski

Arthur Yorinks and Richard Egielski first collaborated on Sid and Sol *(1977), which Maurice Sendak described as "a wonder."* Louis the Fish *was named one of the Best Books of 1980 by* School Library Journal; It Happened in Pinsk *was a Booklist Children's Editors' Choice for 1984, and* Hey, Al *won the 1987 Caldecott Medal.* Buz, *illustrated and written by Richard Egielski is one of his latest, most successful titles. A sample of his illustration appears on page 122.*

GETTING PUBLISHED

After I graduated from Parsons School of Design, I would occasionally visit my former instructor, Maurice Sendak. I showed him my work and complained that I wasn't getting any offers from publishers to illustrate picture books.

Unbeknownst to me, Arthur Yorinks was also visiting Maurice's class. He had shown him several of his manuscripts and complained to Maurice about his lack of offers from publishers. Maurice told Arthur of a former student whose work was very good and would go well with Arthur's stories, but he could not remember the student's last name, so he described him to Arthur and told him that his first name was Richard.

One afternoon I was in the elevator on my way to visit Maurice when someone tapped me on the shoulder and asked if I was Richard.

He introduced himself as Arthur Yorinks and said that Maurice Sendak had told him about me. He asked if I would like to see some of his stories. So in an empty classroom that day I read *Sid and Sol*. It was to be our first book published by Farrar, Straus and Giroux.

That fateful meeting in the elevator of Parsons brought us together as an author/illustrator team and our careers began.

Richard Peck

Richard Peck, who was born in Decatur, Illinois, was the 1990 recipient of the Margaret A. Edwards Award for the body of his young adult fiction. He has received the National Council of English/ALAN Award, the 1991 Medallion from the University of Southern Mississippi, and the Edgar Allan Poe Award for the Are You in the House Alone? *His nonfiction book for writers and teachers is* Love and Death at the Mall: Teaching and Writing for the Literate Young *(1994). Four of his novels have been made into feature-length films. The cover of* Ghosts I Have Been *appears on page 121.*

HOW I FIRST CAME TO BE PUBLISHED

Teaching made a writer out of me. Teaching raised that question that has to be answered before putting pen to paper: "Who are the people who might be willing to read what I might be able to write?"

I found those people in my rollbook. They were my students, the people I knew best and liked best, and from our first hours together I'd learned things about them their parents dared never know. It wasn't the seniors. From me the

seniors wanted only glowing recommendations to college, fiction of a sort now that I come to think of it. It wasn't anybody in high school who made a novelist out of me.

That happened in junior high where I'd been reassigned as an English teacher. One day I looked around, and I was the only one in the room not going through puberty. Worse, none of the curricula of high school applied here. Puberty has always been the great unknown and the reading list a problem. You can get just so much mileage out of *The Red Pony*.

Poetry was another problem. I'd passed my own puberty with the good gray poets of New England, committing long stretches of Longfellow to heart, under the teacher's direction. This didn't work either.

But short poetry is too useful in a classroom to be abandoned. I began to excise from magazines and anthologies contemporary poems on issues I hoped my students couldn't deny. I (illegally) reproduced them on sheets and did a daily poetry delivery. Some of the poems worked, and I saved them. My file grew. I arranged thematically because that's what English teachers do. "Let's make a book out of our favorite poems," I said, and it became a unit, one I could update for future semesters.

All this was happening in New York City. I carried that collection down to a paperback publisher and asked for an interview with the editor-in-chief of the juvenile books department. At the end of the 1960s paperback publishers were looking for classroom inroads. "Would other teachers find this collection useful?" the editor asked, and I said I thought they would, if it could be priced in the fifty-cent range. That collection became *Sounds & Silences*, and out of print ever since.

But the novel lies near the English teacher's heart, perhaps nearest. Finding the novel my puberty people could and would read, the novel that spoke straight to them, became the ultimate challenge. It occurred to me that the books I assigned them were snubbing them. No writer I knew of was speaking to them, though Judy Blume and S.E. Hinton were even then bursting upon the scene.

I quit my job one day, May 24, 1971. I turned in my tenure and went home to try to write just one novel my former students couldn't call irrelevant. Unemployment focuses the mind, I knew I couldn't be Judy Blume or S.E. Hinton. And my students had warned me against autobiography. I was heavy-burdened with all the things I couldn't do as I sat at the desk, tinkering with opening paragraphs. I knew the main character would be a high school freshman because my students were chiefly interested in people two years older. I knew it couldn't be set in the school I'd just left because I was still too close to it. After six drafts the book became *Don't Look and It Won't Hurt*, still in print a quarter century later and filmed in the 1990s as *Gas, Food, Lodging*.

Because of the poetry collection, I knew where to take it. An editor of the paperback publisher was now the juveniles editor-in-chief of a hardback publisher. I took the novel manuscript to him, hoping for advice. He called the next morning, saying, "You may start your second novel." That was twenty-five years and twenty-five books ago.

Had I mailed the manuscript to a publishing house without addressing it to the person in charge, had I not made some kind of contact in advance with him, I believe I would have got that manuscript back – then or now. Was it easier to get a first novel published in 1971? Probably not. YA was a much narrower field. Librarians weren't taking courses in the young adult novel. The English teachers hadn't yet founded the ALAN organization to promote these novels in the classroom. It's never easy to begin. I believe my first novel found a publisher because it was about the readers, not the author. We don't write what we know. We write what we wonder about. Now I sit at the backs of other teachers' classrooms, trying to learn more about the people I hope will read the books I haven't written yet.

Joan Lowery Nixon

Nixon's books have won many awards, including four Edgars from Mystery Writers of America, two Spur awards from Western Writers of America, and seventeen children and young adult choice awards in a number of states. "But," she says, "the greatest reward has been the letters I've received from young people in middle school or junior high who took the step from being reluctant readers to avid readers because of my books. As one ninth-grade girl put it: 'Thank you for the gift of reading.' This is the finest and most welcome award a writer can receive."

In 1997, Nixon's books will include a young adult mystery, Murdered, My Sweet; Circle of Love, *the seventh book in* The Orphan Train Adventures; Make a Wish, *the first book in the spin-off* Orphans Train Children *series for ages seven to eleven (all Bantam Doubleday Dell); and two books for ages seven to eleven in* The Casebusters *series for Disney Press. The cover of* A Family Apart *appears on page 121.*

WRITING AND PUBLISHING MY FIRST BOOK

I began writing professionally when I was seventeen and sent a short article to *The Ford Times*. I received a check for thirty-five dollars and thought, "Wow! This beats baby-sitting!" For years I wrote for magazines – some fiction, but mostly nonfiction: *Baby Talk*, *American Home*, *Parents*, *Woman's Day* and many company and religious magazines.

By 1961 I wasn't writing because I was busy with our four small children. However, we had recently moved to Corpus Christi, Texas, which hosted a major writers' conference each year. Determined to get back to writing, I attended the conference.

That evening I told my husband and children that I had heard two people speak about writing for children, and the idea was intriguing. Our two oldest daughters, who were in elementary school, came to me later and said, "Mommie, we've decided. If you're going to write for children, you have to write a book, it has to be a mystery, and you have to put us in it."

Corpus Christi also hosted a major hurricane that summer, so I began to develop a plot based on two girls and their little brother who are accidentally left behind when a beach area is evacuated because of an approaching hurricane.

Writing is a craft as well as an art, so I knew there must be rules about writing for children. Unfortunately, there were no local courses taught in the subject; but our librarian gave me a copy of Phyllis Whitney's book about how to write for children, and I practically memorized Miss Whitney's good advice.

My mother telephoned and said, "I want to see you get back to writing, so I'll stake you to a cleaning woman one day a week for a year. Have her watch the little ones so you can shut yourself up in your bedroom and write."

That was one of the best gifts I've ever received. It gave me the opportunity to write without interruption, and it demanded discipline. On Wednesdays – my writing days – I didn't let anything interfere with my time to write.

I began by writing articles and short stories – some of them for magazines like *'Teen* and the Scholastic Magazines, and kept working on the plan for my mystery novel. After six months I told my mother that I was earning enough from my magazine pieces to take over the cleaning woman's salary, but my mother insisted, "I promised an entire year. Just keep writing." So I began writing my book.

Each Wednesday afternoon, after I picked up our two

older children from school, all four of them would sit at my feet and say, "Now, read."

They were good critics. If they got wiggly, I knew that I'd have to put more suspense or action in that particular spot. And they'd tell me exactly what they thought. After I'd finished reading one particular chapter, Kathy, our sixth-grader, said, "That was too scary for too long, Mommie. Put in something funny." So I went back through all that I had written and added "natural humor" – things their four-year-old brother character would do or say, being a typical four-year-old.

By the end of the year I had finished the first draft of my mystery novel, which I had planned for the eight-to-twelve age group, and I called it *The Mystery of Hurricane Castle*.

After a great deal of writing, rewriting and polishing, I entered the manuscript in Corpus Christi's 1962 writers' conference and won first prize in the juvenile book division. That gave me the confidence to submit the manuscript to publishers. After studying countless books geared to ages eight-to-twelve in the library and buying a copy of *Writer's Market*, I made a list of publishers who might be interested in a mystery for readers aged eight-to-twelve.

Going down the list, I sent my manuscript out thirteen times. The first twelve publishers rejected it – sometimes with an encouraging letter, sometimes with a printed rejection slip. Then, to my delight, the editor at Criterion, the thirteenth publishing house, accepted the manuscript with great enthusiasm.

Why did I keep persisting in submitting my manuscript after the first few rejections? Because I believed in it. I knew it was a good story.

Was it rejected because it wasn't a good book? Of course not. I knew there were many reasons for rejections that had nothing to do with the quality of my book. *The Mystery of Hurricane Castle* proved itself. It was bought for paperback reprint, it was a Calling All Girls book club selection, and a section of the book was later chosen as an SRA reading selection.

The book was published in 1964, and I recently celebrated the publication of my one-hundredth book. Writing demands courage, persistence, determination and a great deal of hard work; but to my way of thinking, it's the best job in the world.

Katie Lee's success story on page 94 gives these jackets and illustrations a special significance by showing how talent plus persistence leads to success.

A pencil sketch and finished watercolor, preliminary studies for *A Visit to Galapagos*.

❧ THE GANDER ❧

Be careful not to cross the gander,
A bird composed of beak and dander.
His heart is filled with prideful hate
Of all the world except his mate,
And if the neighbors do not err
He's overfond of beating her.
Is she happy? What's the use
Of trying to psychoanalyze a goose?

A sketch and double-page spread from
Underwater With Ogden Nash.

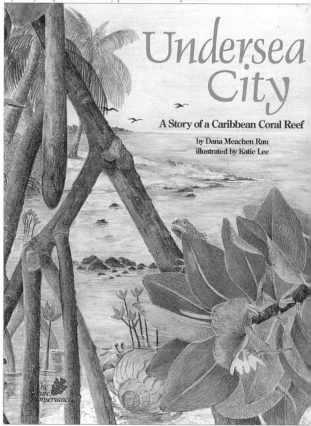

Jacket for *Undersea City.*

Preliminary study and final artwork for a double page spread from *Undersea City*.

Here is a lesson plan demonstrating the use of children's fiction in the classroom:

When Liz Amoss' seventh grade class lost interest in *The Old Man and the Sea*, the students were told that they would be working on a parody of three separate works: the novel itself, either the Noah or the Jonah story, and the enclosed folding storybook cards. The texts would borrow from biblical style, with inverted subject and verb order. Students were reminded to make use of colors, simile, personification, and every other literary device on which the class focused during the year. The class could take liberties with setting and selected details.

The second step of the assignment was to design appropriate and playful titles and cover illustrations, framed by meaningful borders, in the format of the folding storybook cards.

One of the storybook cards, *Jonah*, illustrated by Berthe Amoss, which was used as the basis for the lesson plan. The story and illustration are revealed as the card unfolds.

Here is text and artwork by some of the students.

*"Now, upon the eighty-fifth day of horrible luck, the Jo DiMaggio said
   unto the old man: 'Arise, to the great sea, go you must.'
And a swift* brisa *the lord sent. Farther, farther across* la mar *Santiago
   was summoned, until the lights of Havana behind him shone no longer."*
– Lindsey Koretsky, Seventh Grade, Isidore Newman School

*"Then, the Great Galano shark, sent by the lord to shun Santiago,
   emerged from the waves and sent a spray all over the sea, as if angels
   from above were dumping pails of the lord's rage down on Earth.
The tremendous current threw Santiago out of the boat, and the Great
   Galano swallowed his human bait."*
– Brian Rosenblatt, Seventh Grade, Isidore Newman School

Chuck Galey, whose essay appears on page 97, contributed this demonstration based on his workshop for the Children's Book Festival at the University of Southern Mississippi in Hattiesburg, February, 1997.

#3) This is a quick value sketch of the large bugs. Also, the design of the illustration continues to develop.

#1) I always begin an illustration with small "thumbnail" sketches. Here is a progression of ideas in which I show large bugs chasing a couple of kids who like to collect bugs.

#4) After transferring the line drawing to the illustration board, I've worked ou a small color thumbnail drawing which will help when painting the finished art Here, acrylic paint is used to block in some of the background color.

#2) This is a close-up development of the two characters. I've created a value sketch by shading in areas and making color notes. Small lead weights are used to help hold sketches in place.

#5) Continuing to block in the background color, I begin to work in some of the main elements in the illustration. This work goes quickly as I've already decided on the color scheme from the small color thumbnail. ▮▪▪▶

114

#6) Here, detail work begins on the big bugs and the escaping children.

#9) Although the bugs are larger, the children are more intense in value and hue. Your eyes go directly to them first, then you discover the big bugs. Here, more detail is added to the children.

#7) At this stage of the illustration, I've created an oil wash, a mixture of purple and green. This creates a neutral blue. When this dries, I go back in with a kneaded eraser and pull out highlights. This helps to give the illustration a cool image with depth.

#10) Finally, the small detail work is finished and a clean, crisp image is left to visually tell a part of the story.

#8) As you can see the main characters of the illustration are beginning to show more detail. As designed in the initial sketches, I wanted the viewer's eye to first go to the fleeing children.

Soon the other guests arrived with presents and treats to share. The house was festive with decorations, gaily wrapped gifts, and the merry chatter of the children.
"I want to light the first candle!" squealed Melly.
"I want to open the first present!" cried Tess.
"I want to eat the first latke!" boomed Benny.
"I want us all to have a happy Hanukkah!" said Uncle Jack.

Planning a book with a novelty feature takes advance planning, knowledge of the format and manufacturing process, and mastery of the special technical needs of the printer. Stickers are a relatively simple but popular "novelty" in picture books for preschoolers. In planning her Hanukkah book, *Melly's Menorah,* Amye Rosenberg had to provide original color artwork, seen here, for more than fifty full-color stickers to be bound into the book.

Amye knew that a die-cutting machine would cut around the shape of each sticker so the reader could easily peel it from the page. In order to provide a guide for the machine – a sort of mechanical cookie cutter – Amye provided a separate transparent overlay with a black ink line around each sticker. She was aware that she had to leave white space around each tiny picture, so the die-cutter would not slice off any important pictorial element.

In the final book, the black line did not print. But the guide had done its job of ensuring that each sticker maintained its integrity.

As one of the distinctive features of the book, Amye provided a picture on the back cover that children can complete as the eight days of Hanukkah progress. By peeling and placing stickers in the picture of a menorah, children can reenact the Hanukkah ritual without matches! When planning this portion of the book, Amye had to provide accurate outlines showing correct placement of the stickers.

A Happy Hanukkah Book

WITH OVER 50 FULL-COLOR PEEL-OFF STICKERS!

Place a Shammas sticker in the center holder, then "light" another candle on each of the eight nights of Hanukkah.

A LITTLE SIMON BOOK
Published by Simon & Schuster

The artist's work is never done. Joan Elizabeth Goodman worked and reworked her pictures for *Good Night, Pippin* throughout the submission and publication process. She sold the book to Golden on the strength of her complete book of pencil sketches. Nevertheless, after acceptance she submitted a second complete sketch dummy reflecting subtle changes in perspective, rendering and mood. The successful artist uses every opportunity to improve the book.

Here we see an early color sample for the book. Note that Joan has created a picture with old-fashioned charm through the use of flat color and a placid mood.

In the finished book, Joan used essentially the same composition but added richer, more modulated color and eye-catching details. The finished product is more dramatic and a better vehicle for Joan's superb storytelling.

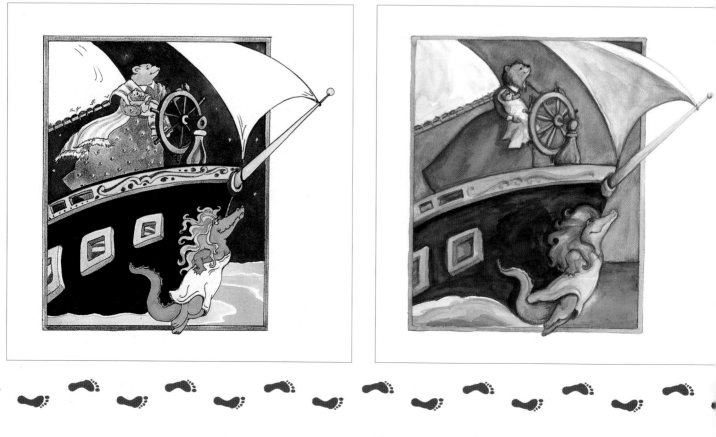

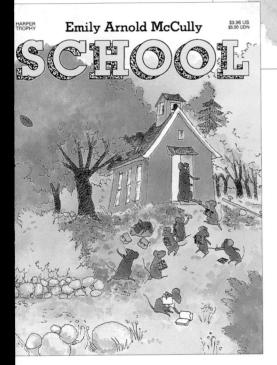

Emily Arnold McCully's essay on getting started in publishing appears on page 98. Shown here are illustrations from *School*, a wordless book. The jacket from *The Bobbin Girl*, recently published, shows how much her style has changed.

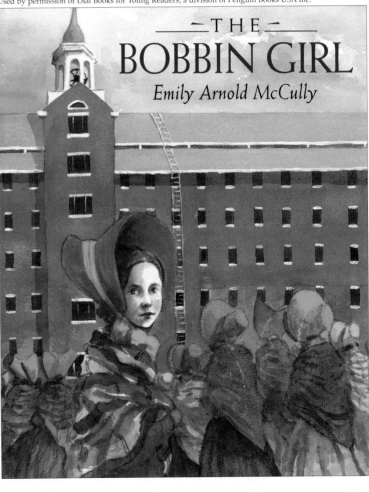

For Santa

Mike Artell's illustrations in *The Night Before Christmas* are collages made from torn paper. His *Legs* is a lift-the-flap book. His success story appears on page 99.

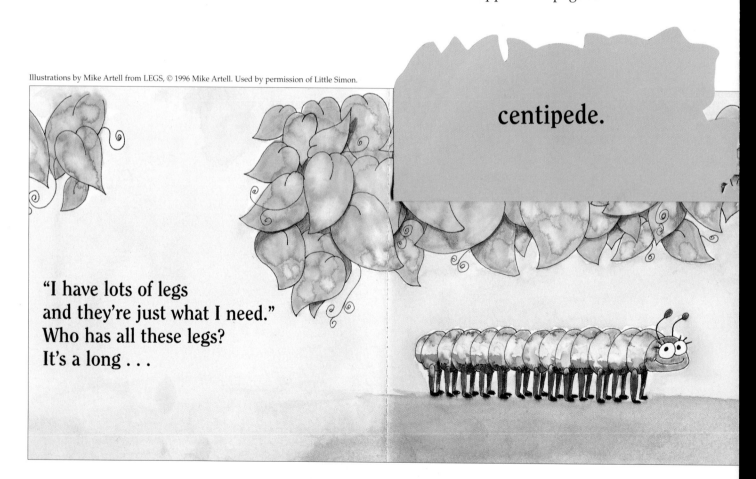

centipede.

"I have lots of legs
and they're just what I need."
Who has all these legs?
It's a long . . .

Richard Peck's popular books are on-going. Pictured here is the jacket of one of his earliest and most successful books. His essay is on page 105.

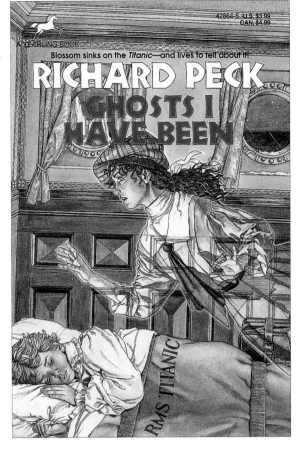

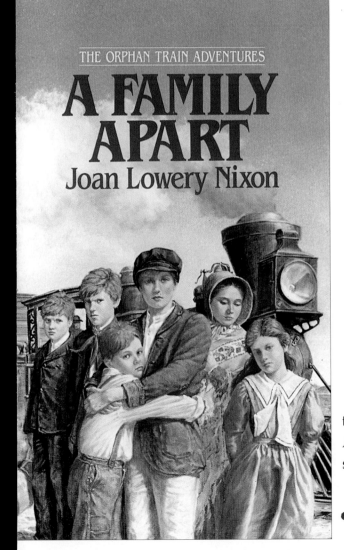

Among Joan Lowery Nixon's many popular titles, the Orphan Train Adventure series, based on American history, stands out. Her inspiring success story is on page 107.

"I'm quitting your service, I've had quite enough
of your three-legged thistles asleep in my wash,
of scrubbing the millstone you use for a dish,
and riding to shops on a pickle-winged fish."

"Pish, posh,"
said Hieronymus Bosch.

Pish, Posh, Hieronymus Bosch, written by Nancy Willard and illustrated by the Dillons, is discussed on page 42.

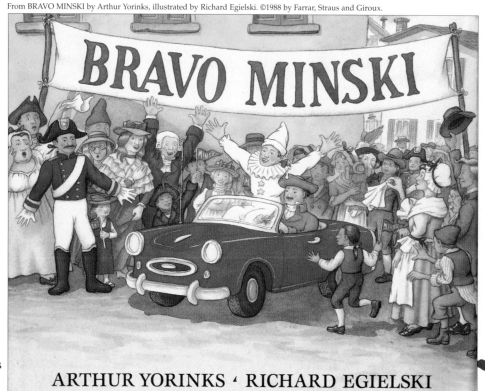

Richard Egielski's delightful essay, found on page 105, proves that serendipity plays a role in success.

From AUNG SAN SUU KYI, by Whitney Stewart, cover photograph by
G. Fenmore. Used by permission of Lerner Publications Company.

The jacket of Whitney Stewart's timely biography is sure to attract the attention of young people. Her story is on page 95.

Illustration by Margot Tomes reprinted by permission of Coward-McCann, Inc from WHAT'S THE
BIG IDEA, BEN FRANKLIN? by Jean Fritz, illustrations copyright © 1976 by Margot Tomes.

One of Jean Fritz's biographies which inspired Whitney Stewart and changed the way biography is presented to young people.

Lisbeth Zwerger's art straddles the border between illustration and fine art. For more about the artist, see Step 4, Seeing the Book as an Art Form.

CASE HISTORY (BERTHE)

Eric and I had completed this book, it had been edited, and we were waiting for our graphic designer, Rebecca Blake, to return from abroad. I took a week-long intensive course in botanical illustration from Katie Lee and knew we had to include her work in our book for two reasons: her illustration is outstanding and her case history fantastic. Amazingly, she had taught herself everything and become successful in eight years. Next, I realized that another of my most favorite illustrators, Roberto Innocenti, (A Christmas Carol, Pinocchio) is also self-taught. Then came the "aha!" insight: we are all self-taught! Most of us have writing and art instruction and we read how-to books, but in the end, it is what we do alone in our work places that teaches us and spells success. And so, dear Reader, we thank you for reading our book, and we wish you great good luck with yours.

The End